THE RICHEST VILLAGE IN ENGLAND

History of Kessingland
Part 2

Kessingland Beach.

Peter Cherry

Edited by Betty Cherry and Maureen Long

THE RICHEST VILLAGE IN ENGLAND

Cover Design
KT PUBLICATIONS

First Published 2005 by
K.T. Publications,
52 London Road, Kessingland,
Lowestoft, Suffolk, NR33 7PW
TEL: 01502 740 539

I.S.B.N. 0 9539046   5 2

Printed by Rondor Printing Co Limited
Lorne Park Rd., Lowestoft, Suffolk NR33 0RD
Tel 01502 564860

Typesetting: K.T. Publications

INTRODUCTION AND ACKNOWLEDGEMENTS

After the success of the first part of the Kessingland History trilogy: - *From Stoneage to Stagecoach,* we are pleased and proud to bring you Part 2, entitled *The Richest Village in England,* containing more of the late Peter Cherry's articles, first published in *the Kessingland and Broadland Times,* from the *Lowestoft Journal* and the *Eastern Daily Press,* by kind permission of Peter Frantzen, Editor, *Eastern Counties Newspapers, (now Archant).*

We acknowledge with gratitude the hard work put into this book by Mrs. Betty Cherry and family, who are as eager as we are to see a comprehensive history of Kessingland from Peter's past writing and his vast collection of old postcards and photographs. Acknowledgements and thanks also to the family of the late Trevor Westgate, for excerpts from *The Roaring Boys,* written by Peter and Trevor.

Thanks are also due to the Staff at Rondor Printing Company, for their expertise and co-operation in the production of this book.

We look forward to publishing the final part of this history before too long, which will contain Peter's record of notable village events in the twentieth century.

This part accurately and evocatively describes much of Kessingland's rich fishing industry, when the village was dubbed *The Richest Village in England,* giving us the title for this book, which also pays tribute to those brave Kessingland fishermen and life-boatmen, who gave their skill and often their lives for the industry. That, and the sacrifices of their families, is the true cost of fish!

We are honoured to publish this book in theirs and Peter's memory.

Maureen and Eric Long, *K.T. Publications,* September 2005

KESSINGLAND'S PIONEERS OF STEAM

When the port at Kessingland silted up and was finally blocked around 1600 it meant the end of an era of prosperity - based on its herring fleet - going back to Saxon times. This had been a community of fishermen, many of them prosperous boat owners. No doubt fishing continued with boats putting off from the beach, as Lowestoft fishermen had done down the ages before the creation of a harbour in the 19th century.

By 1777 even this limited fishing from Kessingland Beach seems to have died out. The Rev. John Arrow informed his bishop that the parish then contained "About 45 houses and 251 inhabitants who exercise themselves in agriculture." Significantly he made no mention of fishermen.

It was not until Lowestoft harbour was completed in 1831 that the herring fishing again began to boom, so much so that the docks proved inadequate to cope with the press of drifters and trawlers. Eventually a new dock, the Waveney, had to be hurriedly excavated. It was during this expansion that Kessingland men began to return to their old calling as herring fishermen - and fine seamen they proved to be.

They would return home after the Autumn voyage with their pockets jingling with golden sovereigns. Those were the days of sail, but it was not long before Kessingland men began to pioneer the building of the first steam drifters. Mr George 'Mouse' Catchpole, William Tripp and Messrs C and R Harvey were among the Kessingland boat owners who led the way, 'Mouse' ordering the building of the first steam drifter, *Consolation,* from the yard of Chambers and Colby in 1897 - over a 100 years ago. As more and more steam drifters were built the scene was set for the greatest East Anglian herring fishing of all time. This came in 1913 when there were nearly 2000 drifters at sea - 1600 of them steamers. "The scene at night was like some fantastic fairy land," was how one fisherman described it, "Myriads of red and green navigation lights and thousands of acetylene deck lights flooded the seas and glowed into the skies, paling the strongest moonlight." That herring fishing of 1913 was an amazing bonanza - what would 1914 bring? It brought the First World War! Instead of shooting their nets in search of the herring, the fishermen were out on patrol seeking out the mines and - in some cases casting their nets to ensnare German submarines! It was Kessingland boat owner William Tripp who suggested to the Admiralty that the fishing boats could catch the subs as effectively as they netted herrings. Experiments proved successful and lanes of nets were laid from England to France enabling troop ships to pass through safely.

The Lowestoft Journal reported: "The valuable services Mr Tripp rendered were brought to the notice of the King by the Admiralty and his Majesty conferred upon him the M.B.E."

There was never to be another herring voyage like that of 1913, but, despite ups and downs, good seasons and poor, the herring fishing continued to provide prosperity for many fishermen - and to draw all and sundry to the quayside to watch the herring baskets being swung ashore - and to gather in a generous share of the bounty!

So many, indeed, crowded on to the fish market that, early in 1962, the Docks Board decided to close the market to the general public and to enclose it with steel railings.

It was the enterprise of Kessingland boat owners in pioneering the steam drifters and the skill and prosperity of its fishermen which led to the village acquiring the nickname 'Klondyke' and the reputation of being 'The richest village in England' - perhaps something of an exaggeration - but it was certainly a very well-to-do place.

In those days there was no public transport so they had to trudge miles to board their vessels. The roads were so bad that most of them walked along the beach. They certainly earned their money!

Scotch fisher girls barrelling the cured herrings on the quayside ready for export

EARLY TRANSPORT

It was around a hundred years ago, in July 1904, that Kessingland welcomed its first bus service. It had been introduced by the Great Eastern Railway, which ran a service from Lowestoft to Southwold, stopping off at Kessingland. The object of the G.E.R. was to link up via the Southwold Railway, with the mainline route to London. reaching the capital in two and a half hours (better than today!) The buses were open-topped Milne's Daimlers. The fact that the roads were in an atrocious condition and the buses were equipped with solid tyres, did not make for a very comfortable journey, plus the fact that the upper deck was open to the elements. But it was a first for Kessingland as well as the G.E.R., for this was the first provincial bus service in the country! Earlier, in 1898, Kessingland had had high hopes of a light railway running a regular service to Kessingland Beach. This had been proposed by the East Anglian Light Railway Co., and was planned to run from Caister, through Lowestoft to Kessingland. There were, around this time, a number of proposals for a Kessingland line,

notably the Great Eastern Railway, which was also interested in such a line. Then there was the idea of a tramway from the Royal Plain to our village and another was for the Southwold Railway to run a track north to Kessingland. What with objections from various interested parties, and the expense, none of these plans ever came to fruition and our hopes for a railway station here came to nought.

Meanwhile the Southwold Railway, which ran through Walberswick,

Blythburgh and Wenhaston to Halesworth, continued to attract passengers, the affection of the town and many bizarre stories, some true but others dismissed as myths. There was the story, for instance, of a small circus paying a visit to Southwold which sent its young lion ahead on the railway, the charge amounting to £8, which was not forthcoming. The caged lion was therefore housed in the waiting room at the station, to be held until payment was made. The lion did not go hungry. The Station handyman was dispatched to the nearest butcher to buy a shillings-worth of cheap meat. This was gingerly fed to the lion on the end of a very long pole. So as not to alarm passengers, the cage was covered with a tarpaulin whenever a train was due. Fortunately the circus did well and was soon able to pay its dues. There was also the legend that much of this railway was from the Woo Sung and Shanghai railway in China, which, having proved uneconomical was ripped up and much of it thrown into the river. It was later salvaged and was shipped back to this country where it was claimed, it ended up as part of the Southwold Railway. Experts insist that this story was nothing but myth, but there was some evidence that there could have been another China connection. The Bristol Tramway & Carriage Co. was said to have built and shipped out to China a number of carriages, but when these proved unsatisfactory, they were shipped back to this country and were adapted for the Southwold Railway. There was a great deal of regret when Southwold Railway finally closed on April 11th. 1929, but the local myths continued to be popular. To mark the closure a local newspaper printed a farewell poem:

Southwold Railway's gone to pot,
Where it was, it now is not.
No good making any fuss.
Come to Ipswich; take a bus.
Southwold lies in isolation,
Though it has a railway station,
But alas, no trains will run
Lookers-on enjoy the fun.

The various plans for light railways having fallen through, Lowestoft decided to embark on its own tram service, running from the Royal Plain to Pakefield. Work started on March 11th. 1903, and the service ran successfully until the final closure in May 1931, being replaced by a Corporation bus service. Lowestoft trams also seem to have had their problems with circus managers and animals. A baby elephant was among the unusual passengers on the trams. It was conveyed on a specially-strengthened tram from Pakefield to Station Square for the adults single fare of tuppence. The baby elephant seems to have caused little trouble on the ride, but that was certainly not the case when a Circus Master boarded the tram at Pakefield with his dancing bear. Both Master and bear were directed to the upper deck, crowded at the time but very soon cleared, as the Circus Master struck up a tune on his concertina and the bear danced a jig. The crew of the tram were somewhat perplexed as to the price of the fare for a bear, but decided to charge that for a dog-tuppence. Back at the depot there were some hard words for the crew, which was informed that bears were not to be regarded as dogs!

THE ROARING BOYS

The fishermen of the Suffolk coast, whether they put to sea in the modern powerful vessels of Lowestoft's fishing fleet the fifth biggest in Great Britain or in little longshore boats from some small creek or open beach, are a race apart. They are a race of men in whose veins the blood of the Vikings still courses; barrel-chested men who live their lives with gusto, men with gargantuan appetites for the sea, fish and beer!

They are probably the finest seamen to be found anywhere in the North Sea and seldom does catastrophe strike without at least one Lowestoft fishing boat arriving on the scene and they are often the first to give aid. In past years they have gained more awards for their daring and gallant rescues than men of any other port which gets its living from the North Sea.

The ships may have changed over the centuries, but it still requires skill, courage and fortitude to fight the sea for a living. And when they come ashore, they celebrate with the same robust vigour.

They are, indeed, "The Roaring Boys of Suffolk" as they became known in the 17th century. The name comes, not from their uproarious way of life, but from one of the jobs of the fishermen in those days. Before ice was generally available the only way of preserving herring was to sprinkle them with salt. The piles of fish were turned over with a blunt-edged, wooden shovel, known as a "roaring shovel". The operation was known as "roaring" and those who did it were called "roaring boys".

In time, the name seems to have been applied to all fishermen and finally spread to London where ruffians or noisy bands of youngsters were derided as "roaring boys" or "Mohawks".

But the true "roaring boys" were fishermen and the most famous were those of Pakefield celebrated in the ancient rhyme:

"The Roaring Boys of Pakefield
"They didn't know what to contrive
"They had only one poor parson
"And him they buried alive."

History does not tell us why they buried their parson, but it is said that he was found drunk on the beach and for a bit of fun they buried him up to his neck in the sands!

Later poets added more verses elaborating on the legend. The Roaring Boys also figured in another rhyme which appeared below a painting of a shipwreck in the Ship Inn at Pakefield now. alas, beneath the waves:

> She strikes the sand, she parts the deck
> The crew now float upon the wreck
> But safe from harm God guards the strand
> And keeps his Roaring Boys at hand.

These, then, were the Roaring Boys the fishermen of Suffolk. And when the gale blows or the beer flows their descendants can still roar with the best of them.

FISH NAMED JIM!

The North Sea is a shallow sea, and one which is intensively fished over by all the nations bordering it. Anything which goes into the sea usually comes up again sooner or later in the meshes of the great trawl nets which hundreds of trawlers drag across the bottom.

The imperishable bric-a-brac of countless voyagers the wine jug hurled overboard by a 16th century reveller, or the empty bottle consigned to the deep by his 20th century counterpart, rise from the depths to thump down on the deck of a modern trawler.

Mammoths' teeth, or their great tusks, may lie in peat beds beneath the sea for 60,000 years before they, too, see the light of day again on the deck of a Lowestoft trawler. Great anchors lost in the gales of yesteryear, many dating back to the days of Nelson and before, finally surface entangled in the fishing nets. The wrecks of long forgotten ships rust and decay to strew their cargo on the sea-bed this, too, eventually finds its way into the catch of a trawler

All these, though of great interest to the archaeologist and the geologist, are just a nuisance to the Lowestoft fishermen who are interested in seeing only one thing in their nets fish.

But there are more deadly things still waiting on the bed of the North Sea for the nets of innocent fishermen mines, bombs and torpedoes from two world wars. They are the things which the trawlermen fear rusty barnacle-encrusted relics which slide ominously out of the cod-end to go bump on the deck. Then there is a quick, panicky rush to rope it securely to the rail before it can roll about the deck. A hurried radio call and the trawler turns for home where a bomb disposal squad will be waiting.

But there are trawlers which never make it back to port with their dangerous cargo, trawlers which disappear at sea in fine weather, no question of their having been lost in a storm. They are the victims of mines or depth charges which exploded as soon as they hit the deck. Two Lowestoft trawlers lost since the war, *Susan M* and *SDJ,* are believed to have been the victims of such catches. Precisely how they were lost will never be known, but it is thought that they were quietly fishing when they trawled up an old mine or a depth charge. Either it detonated as the trawl swung alongside the ship or when the cod-end was opened to disgorge the catch on to the deck. Their end was sudden, violent and mysterious.

No wonder then that Lowestoft fishermen treat with the utmost respect anything that goes bump on the deck and when that bump is a mine, handle it with kid gloves till they can get back to port.

Why undertake this dangerous trip, sometimes hundreds of miles, back to port with what amounts to a time bomb ticking away on deck? Why not throw it back into the sea as quickly as possible? These are questions which are asked by many a landsman. The answers are simple. Anything thrown into the North Sea will eventually be trawled up again and that applies to mines too! And the next time it hits the deck they may not be so lucky, it may blow up immediately. And throwing it back may prove even more dangerous than keeping it securely lashed on deck.

The trawler *Boston Pegasus* was unlucky enough a few years after the war to trawl up an old rusty drum in its trawl. It looked harmless enough, indeed, everyone thought it was just an old drum. "Throw it over the side," shouted the skipper and over it went. Seconds later, its fuse actuated as it sank through the water, the depth charge blew up, smashing the trawler's wheelhouse windows and putting her electrical systems out of action. It was a narrow escape and one which made skippers even more reluctant to throw anything back into the sea.

Magnetic mines, acoustic mines and the conventional horned contact mines were all laid in the North Sea by the Royal Navy and the German Navy during the second world war. There are still areas which have not been swept clear, and probably they never will be. In the great storms and surges of the North Sea some break loose to add to the harvest of death on the seabed. Some of the mines which have been brought up date back over half a century to the first world war and they are still deadly!

The fishermen of Lowestoft know them well. In two world-wars, when the town was the base for the Royal Navy's mine-sweeping service, they used their skill to sweep the convoy channels off the east coast. They know their mines and how treacherous they can be.

Even so, they sometimes treat them in cavalier fashion, like the skipper who rendered a mine "harmless" by sawing off the horns a procedure guaranteed to blow him and his ship to Kingdom Come had he not been lucky enough to use his hacksaw on an absolute dud! The mine disposal expert to whom he proudly showed his handiwork gave him quite a severe talking to when he had got his breath back!

Even ashore the east coast fishermen are not safe from the relics of war. In 1968, unexploded shells fired into Lowestoft when the German battle cruisers bombarded the town in 1916 came to light during the digging of a sewer. Fifty years had elapsed since they left the muzzles of the German squadron, but their explosive charges were as dangerous as ever. When they were exploded on the outskirts of the town the bang was heard by villagers 12 miles away!

One Lowestoft skipper had a novel and money-making way of dealing with a mine. Sighting a horned mine floating at sea, and remembering that there was a £5 reward for them, he ordered the small boat away and rowed over to it with a coil of rope. He made the rope fast to the mine and then had it hauled on board. "The owner got the reward of £5," he recalled, "and he gave me £1". It hardly seemed worth the risk, but the skipper seemed satisfied!

The dangers of things which are trawled up from the seabed are not always apparent, however. A few years after the second world war, a Lowestoft trawler came back to port with a catch which baffled the crew. It was a strange-looking lump of material which they thought must be a sort of tallow. In the course of their experiments to discover what it was experiments which included tasting it they found that it burned quite readily. Intrigued by this strange stuff, they sent a sample to Norwich Museum. Experts here were also baffled and passed it on to the British Museum. Back came the answer it was gelignite!

Parts of aircraft shot down during the second world war, as well as the bombs which they were carrying, are trawled up from time to time. In September 1966, for instance, *Celita* came back to Lowestoft with the complete engine and propeller of a Shackleton which she had trawled up. It took the crew four hours of hard work to get it on board and there was considerable damage to her nets.

But relics of two world wars are not the only martial bric-a-brac to come to light. Cannon balls and chain shot over two hundred years old have also been found. The prize for antiquity, as far as weapons are concerned, however, must surely go to the prehistoric harpoon which was found by the Lowestoft smack *Colinda* in 1931. It was trawled up on the Leman and Ower bank and was in such perfect condition that one expert described it as looking as though it had just come from a Bond Street shop. Yet it was estimated to be in the region of 9,000 years old, dating back to the days when much of the southern North Sea was land dotted with lakes and the Dogger Bank was covered by pine forests.

At that time, according to geologists, a large river, the remnants of which now form the Rhine, flowed across the plains linking England with the Continent, swinging in a great bend along the present coastline between Kessingland and Cromer. This theory is supported by the bones of mammoths, rhinoceros, sabre-toothed tigers and other animals which have been found preserved in beds of peat.

The pre-historic harpoon, made of bone and about eight inches long, was found in a huge chunk of peat. Known as the "Leman and Ower Harpoon" it is to be seen in Norwich Museum.

These huge chunks of peat "log" as the fishermen call it are of great interest to botanists who have found preserved in them the last vestiges of huge forests traces of oak, alder and pine as well as those of other trees and smaller plant life.

Geologists are also interested in the huge glacial boulders which are found on the seabed. In the early days of large-scale trawling in the North Sea vast quantities of these boulders were hauled up and, because they wanted to clear the fishing grounds, the fishermen invariably brought them back to port. Such huge quantities were landed that they were used as building material and many a house has been built on the firm foundation of glacial boulders. Most of these boulders were cleared years ago, but there are still a few left. In 1952, the Grimsby trawler *Okin* returned to port with one weighing five tons, the biggest ever trawled up.

Grisly relics of wrecks occasionally come up with the fish and an article published in "The Toilers of the Deep" in 1880 tells of one of them:

"More ghastly traces than spars and timbers come up in the trawl far out on this restless sea. The chief engineer of the *Onward,* who is a portly, white-haired person, deliberate of speech and possessing a peculiar bent of humour, keeps suspended in the engine room, behind a cylinder, something which tumbled out of the upbrought net a few days ago, and rolled along the deck.

"That something is a human skull, upon which the barnacles have fastened. Viewing this grim vestige of humanity by the lamp that swung in the casing, the skipper stood beside me and as we turned away, he said: 'That's nothing much, over there on the nor-east Dogger not many months ago, a big ship foundered, and to this day it's common enough for the trawl to bring up the body of a man'."

Such finds were not unusual during the last century when there was a huge loss of life in the North Sea, but they are rare today.

A group of Lowestoft trawlers had an unnerving experience just before the war, however. A famous admiral had been buried at sea and that night a startled skipper hailed the other boats with the news that he had unwittingly fished up the Admiral. He was promptly consigned to his watery grave once more. Then another boat disturbed him again. Six times that night the Admiral returned to the surface and finally the trawlers decided to shift their ground and leave him in peace!

Fortunately such grisly finds are rare, but the North Sea is full of surprises. In February 1969, for instance, Skipper Victor Holmes, in *Boston Valetta,* was intrigued by a weed-covered object which rolled out of the cod-end. After assuring himself that it was not one of those ubiquitous bombs, he took it home to his son Victor, who collects North Sea finds. It proved to be a beautifully-carved African drum. Young Victor added it to his collection which already includes a carved figure in a chair, a dish-washing machine (not working), a selection of ash trays, a number of coffee cups and two dustbins.

Saxon jugs, women's shoes, street signs, prehistoric weapons, a bottle of milk (still fresh!), mammoth's teeth, half a dozen eggs (bad!) and a bicycle. All these have been fished up in recent years. Sometimes these strange catches are dangerous, usually they are nothing but a nuisance. Occasionally they are interesting, but rarely are they worth anything. The fishermen never seem to strike it rich with treasure trove which brings fame and fortune to those who plough the land.

The closest the Lowestoft smacksmen ever came to finding treasure in the deep was probably after the wreck of the German-Lloyd liner *Elbe* in January 1895. She was the crack luxury liner of her day and there was tragic loss of life when she went down in a storm after a collision. The Lowestoft smack *Wildflower* did heroic work in saving many of the survivors. The *Elbe* had on board a great quantity of fine china and as the wreck broke up the sea-bed seems to have been strewn with it, including much still in the original packing cases. One of the loveliest items to be trawled up at that time was an exquisite pair of porcelain figures about a foot high, of a little shepherdess and a fisher-boy. The workmanship is extremely delicate and it is remarkable how they survived being dragged up from the bottom of the sea. A Lowestoft skipper trawled up a packing case of these figures a few years after the disaster and they were distributed among the crew. They are still treasured in a number of local families in which they have been handed down from generation to generation.

Other items of fine china from the *Elbe* are also treasured by Lowestoft families. A Pakefield man. Mr. Sidney Moore, has a teapot, decorated in vivid blue and puce, which he found on the beach not far from his home in the early 1900s. Its similarity to other china from the *Elbe* leaves little doubt that this, too, came from the wreck.

There are a number of very fine moustache cups. too, which came from the wreck. Mr. Roy Roth, of Lowestoft, has a particularly fine one. The cup is always admired by visitors to his home, but most of them are puzzled as to its use. They can scarcely believe that the Victorians had cups with a special shield to protect their precious moustache!

For over 70 years a Lowestoft family has treasured another relic of the *Elbe* a lovely porcelain doll's tea service with a thistle design, still complete and perfect in every detail. The tea service was trawled up by Skipper Bond, one of the leading smack owners of 70 years ago. His family have another interesting relic of the wreck a fine mahogany walking stick with a silver band commemorating the disaster. Chambers' shipyard at Lowestoft made a dozen of these walking sticks from part of a staircase which was washed ashore. They gave one to each of their best customers.

Furniture, fittings, cutlery and china from the *Elbe* all found their way into Lowestoft homes, but perhaps the most staggering haul was that of one Lowestoft skipper who found a grand piano in his nets and managed to get it on board. He took it home with him and contrived to get it into the small parlour of his home.

Though it could scarcely come under the heading of treasure, one Grimsby fisherman has found a profitable little side-line to fishing. He collects lumps of coal which come up with the fish, scrapes the barnacles off and stacks them in a corner. His best trip was seven hundredweight. His theory is that the coal comes from colliers which have sunk, but they may come from out-crops of coal under the sea. Whatever the source, his wife is grateful for the constant supply of fish and coal from a husband who is both fisherman and miner!

Odd as some of these finds have been, even queer things turn up inside the fish themselves. In 1968, for instance, Kessingland longshoreman Victor Knights opened up a cod to find a huge plastic flower inside. "It was quite a shock," he commented. And a cod which was gutted on Lowestoft fish market in October 1967 was found to have half a pound of margarine in its stomach, complete with the wrapping and looking as though it had just come off the shelf of a supermarket!

Cod are what are known as bottom feeders, scraping along the seabed with their lower lip and scooping up anything in their path. Plastic cups, shells, pieces of jewellery and even shoes have been swallowed by the hungry cod. One even contained a knife and fork. But the biggest thing ever found inside one is thought to be half a coconut.

Fishermen are, indeed, almost immune to surprises, but even they were taken aback when a Scottish trawler landed a plaice with its name on its back Jim. The letters were nearly three inches high and it is thought that the plaice had been caught when very small by a fisherman who scratched his name on its back before throwing it back. As the fish grew, so did the letters rather like initials scratched on the bark of a tree.

But the happiest find from the seabed must surely have been the case of champagne which a Lowestoft trawler fished up off the German coast. The champagne was still in fine condition and not a bottle got back to port. The fishermen drank many a toast to whoever had lost it!

DUFF CHOKERS v. PEA BELLIES

The inhabitants of Lowestoft and Yarmouth, have been rivals for hundreds of years indeed, for a considerable period, "enemy" might be a better word. The enmity is now pretty well forgotten but one could hardly call the two places neighbourly. When it was suggested some years ago that the towns should be combined to form a new borough, to be called Yartoft, it was difficult to decide who were the most outraged Lowestoft people or those of Yarmouth!

Lowestoft no longer fights Yarmouth, but there is a certain feeling between them and there are people who cannot bring themselves to mention the name of Yarmouth. If they have to refer to the town they speak of "that other place" or "a place not one hundred miles from here" and everyone knows what they mean. But things are improving. Lowestoft no longer calls Yarmouthians "Duff chokers"or shouts "Jew killer" after the men from Gorleston. In response, people from these towns refrain from sneering "Pea belly" at a Lowestoft man.

No one quite knows why Yarmouth fishermen were known as "Duff chokers" or how the people of Gorleston came to be known as "Jew killers". There is a theory that Gorleston people were said to be so sharp and mean that even a Jew could not get a living in competition with them. But this does not account for the fact that they used to be taunted with the phrase "Who killed the Jew?" There seems to have been some specific Jew involved a Jew foully done to death by the people of Gorleston.

As far as Lowestoft fishermen being called "pea bellies" is concerned we seem to be on a little firmer ground. Historians explain that the fishermen were so poor that they lived chiefly on pea soup and on occasions used to harvest wild sea peas from the denes. This particular type of pea is supposed to have been introduced from a shipwrecked vessel and it is recorded that in 1555 the people of Aldeburgh were saved from starvation during a famine by such a crop.

Certainly peas were an important part of the diet of North Sea fishermen. An account of the running of a herring buss published in 1615 gives details of the victualling of a vessel for 16 men and boys. The equipment included "a large iron pease-pot of five or six gallons" and it was suggested that each member of the crew should be allowed half a pint of peas a day "to be watered and eaten with butter, or else with bacon that is, a gallon a day amongst them all". No wonder the fishermen were called "pea bellies".

It was typical of these fishing communities that they should have nicknames for each other fishermen love a good nickname and it would appear that as soon as a boy was christened they began to look for some odd name with which to saddle him for the rest of his life. It is a tradition which continues to this day. And these nicknames are not the passing schoolboy ones forgotten when school is done. A nickname once acquired by a fisherman sticks for life. Some are even handed down from father to son!

YALLER IRON AND COMPANY

Kessingland is a rare place for nicknames - few people escape without one and very often they are far from flattering! Usually they are acquired from some trivial happening, and then they stick for life. "Yaller Iron" Turrell got his quaint name when, as a lad, he was set to salvage copper bolts from a wreck on the beach. Asked by a coastguard what he was doing, he replied, "I'm just cutting out these little yellow iron bolts." 'Yaller Iron' he remained for the rest of his days!

No one could possibly set down all the nicknames which have befallen Kessingland men down the ages, but one fisherman has given me a remarkable list of those he can remember from his days with the fishing fleet. He lists no fewer than 100 men who were skippers who fished out of Lowestoft. Not all had nicknames, but here are a few of those who did, family by family, though not in alphabetical order.

CATCHPOLE- Truncher, Tidley, Light, Labby, Funk, Sly, Wilky, Pilcher, Boiler, Crop, Trunnie, Bucko, Pardy, Ike, Holele, Nash, Hinix, Hucker, Hundred, Starcher, Mouse, Lando, Dog, Hudge and Ebber.

UTTING / UTTON - Monkey, Yorkie, Deaf Charlie, Twee, Curly, Rusty, Doddles, Shells, Twinie, Moffat, Drug, Rush, Stiff, Braddy, Benny, Yank, Beno, Austy, Nid, Skips, Chy, Peao.

BUNN- Snick, Baze, Swifty, Stilry Poley, Buller, Cockle.

KNIGHTS - Tubby, Backer, Dish, Spuff, Dutch, Wonney, Egger, Ninety, Fritz, Lofty, Cuca, Mum, Sot, Barley, Kruger.

BROWN - Rue, Froggie, Buffer, Hutch, Nanty, Ollie, Dosser, Diddy, Cock Robin, Gobbler.

KEABLE - Friday, Rumbolt, Bighead.

SPILLINGS - Wag, Titler, Brick, Fisher.

STROWGER - Rocks, Gardy, Brewer, Leo, Ossie, Fredadear, Feck, Woops, Tiger, Toots.

MARJORAM - Chips, Manny, Batlie, Hecker, Rollie.

BLOCK - Lallar, Lil, Pum, Pedger.

MALLETT - Hicke.

DOWDING- Tinnie, Dowdy, Milph, Peas, Noisy.

ROTH - Yacker, Stut, Twot.

KEMP - Mike, Beno, Spittems, Turkey, Bumch.

DURRANT - Judy, Dill, Golls, Nossy, Brick.

BLOWERS - Tiff, Woody, Buff, Lue, Micky, Blood, Tash, Cucks, Slater, Gallus.

MUTITT - Tinks, Doff, Rugus, Zip, Pip,

THOMPSON - Ducks, Buffer, Crusty,

HARVEY- Jitty, Skip, Fatty, Youger, Ponto, Billygoat.

SMITH - Ready Money Bob, Boney, Skinny, Bucko, Flipper, Poacher, Bish, Longing, Ducky, Foby.

JAMES - Spider, Whippet.

COOK- Sparkey, Shellie.

BIRD - Stumpy, Bunker, Birdie.

DODDINGTON- Swose, Lar, Doddie, Boler.

MOYSE - Gee, Pots, Hardies, Cuts.

FARROW - Scrub, Mop.

ALDRED - Tin-eye, Chicky, Nolty,

JULINGS- Tager, Greasy, Brush.

TURRELL - Winser, Yellow-Iron, Bark, Jelly, Click, Fluffy, Pouch, Tarrie.

HART - Hufus, Boss, Paddy, Closh, Lodger, Yan.

WIGGS - Hinny, Brownie, Nitty, Hoe.

To complete the list, here are a few odd ones. Haunch Horn, Gunner, Beckham, Tarbrush Cooper, Pilcher Sterry, Ticker Wade, Doey Hall, Marner Weavers, Dumps Davis, Steamboat Thacker, Dutch Sims, Mildew Beamish, Silly Manthorpe, Snuffy Polkard, Onespud Holbrook, Cockerdilly Edwards, Dreamy Smith, Kaiser Bond, Pork Manthorpe, England Reynolds, Toto Robinson, Peck'm Gouldby. Blind Horace.

My apologies to all those quaintly-named characters I have left out. Kessingland is a rare place for a nickname. I can't possibly list them all.

Skipper "Black Eye" Soanes, of Lowestoft, for instance, got his nickname from his father. So did "Rock" Curtis. Skipper Soanes' father got his nickname when he went out with a girl who had a mole on her cheek, just under one eye. "How's your black-eyed girl friend?" his mates used to ask. Eventually, after going out with the girl a few times he found that the nickname "Black Eye" had been foisted upon him. And when he died the name passed to his son, who is still known as "Black Eye".

Another man with a curious nickname was Skipper "Effie" Moore, but he is chiefly remembered not for his odd name, but for his dog Prince who was his constant companion at sea and ashore. Prince, a big, curly-coated black retriever, was always eager to get to sea and would always beat his master and the crew on board the smack. But he was even more eager to get ashore after a trip. As soon as the harbour piers were in sight, Prince would bound over the side and swim ashore. Skipper Moore's wife would always know when the smack was home her husband's return would be heralded by a dripping wet Prince barking at the back gate. Prince had the added distinction of being the only recorded four-legged member of the Royal Antediluvian Order of Buffaloes! Skipper Moore having paid full initiation fees, Prince wore the badge of the order on his collar and sat on his seat in the lodge room of the King Edward VII Lodge in the Great Eastern Hotel in Denmark Road. And he enjoyed his pint as much as his master!

"Rock" Curtis, it is said, got his nickname because he was a hard man and though the characteristic was not passed on to his son, the name was!

There is a wonderful story all the better for a hint of mystery at the end about one member of the Curtis family. He left the little fishing village of Kessingland to go to California to seek his fortune in the gold rush and returned with a small fortune and a nugget of gold the size of a tea-cup. With his money he built himself a house at Kessingland, which he called California House, and a row of cottages, named The Nugget Cottages. They are still to be seen in Church Road.

He also set himself up as a boat owner, calling his first drifter *The Little Nugget*. He prospered greatly and always regarded the nugget of gold as his talisman. When he died the nugget passed to his son and the family felt that as long as the nugget remained with them good fortune would follow. The nugget, according to a member of the family, Mr. John Snelling, a Southwold garage owner, who saw it as a boy, was always brought out on family occasions and birthdays.

"I remember it well being brought across from California House to my mother's house where it would be placed with great ceremony in the middle of the table. It was about the size of a teacup and although it was golden it had a purple sort of sheen to it," says Mr. Snelling. "My uncle always kept the nugget, and treasured it," Mr. Snelling added, "but when he died the nugget was never found. California House was turned upside down, floorboards were taken up and the whole place was ransacked. Not a sign of it could be found in the house or the garden. I still believe that the nugget is hidden somewhere in Kessingland, but no one knows where!"

There is not much doubt about how another man, "Dreepin' Wet," got his nickname. He was the waterman at Lowestoft harbour and going round filling up the tanks of the trawlers was a pretty damp job.

But how did a man get the name "Rubber Heel Irons"? And what possible explanation could there be for the nickname "The white ball peanut"? And one wonders what lies behind the nickname "Tight Skin" Baxter.

Although there is no direct evidence on the subject, the nickname "Steam Whistle" which was given to one Lowestoft fisherman is rather easier to explain. He was probably one of the musical skippers at the port who discovered that they could coax a tune out of the whistles on the new steam vessels.

While not a very musical race, the English like the Scots who produce tunes out of bagpipes delight in getting tunes out of the oddest things. So it was with the steam whistles. Once a skipper had found that, with a little adaptation, he could play tunes on his new steam whistle, there was no stopping them.

Skippers coming back to Lowestoft through the roads would announce their coming with a signature tune, usually a rousing hymn, and the residents at the north end of the town would get the full benefit. Inevitably there were complaints!.

But it was not this which put an end to the musical skippers. The end came when one skipper played "God be with you till we meet again" to a fellow skipper as he steamed out of harbour. They never did meet again the trawler was sunk with all hands. From that moment on there was a distaste and a superstition about playing the whistle. "Steam Whistle" may well have been one of these musical skippers, but like so many, the real origins have been forgotten.

Nicknames were not, of course, confined to the fishermen. Anyone who came into contact with them usually ended up with one. Mr. Adam Adams, Mayor of Lowestoft towards the end of the last century, for instance, was invariably known as "Plummy". He was a grocer by trade and he got his nickname because, anxious to give exact weight and no more, he once cut a plum in half!

A close man was Adam Adams. It is said that when a customer complained that the cheese was full of maggots, he replied, "So it is sir, but they're all cheese, all cheese." This incident led to a move to change his nickname to "Cheesey", but "Plummy" he remained!

What stories lie behind such nicknames as "Come by Chance", "Pig Killer", "Is the Moon Up", "Spit in Hand", "Treacle" or "Cock-a-dilly"? We know that "Poacher" was a fisherman who liked to haul other people's nets and names like "No Finger Meuse" and "Deaf Charlie" are self-evident, but what can one make of the list compiled by one old fisherman of men he knew: "Tardy", "Tantivy", "Brick", "Cor-chick-. "Kaiser", "Dish". "Smell Pot", "The Hero", "Billy Dandy", "Pirn", "Tatoe", "Hulfas". "Yacka", "Pork", "Tar Brush". "Cushoo", "Chuff-Chuff:". "Poker". "Mildew", "Payday" and "Strikes". These are just a few of hundreds of bizarre nicknames which stuck throughout life. Often fishermen are quite unaware of the Christian names and, sometimes, even the surnames of men they have known for years.

As it is with the fishermen, so it is with the fish they catch and the places they frequent all have their odd names.

"I've been standing on Skinner's Know looking for a westerly boat," one lounger once replied when he was asked what he was doing in a particular spot on the fish market. He meant that he was hoping to scrounge a drink! "Waiting for a westerly" meant that he was hoping a drifter would return to port from the westerly fishing. The men on board would have money in their pockets and would, perhaps, buy him a drink. Even today men without anything in their pockets say they are "waiting for a westerly" though that particular fishing died many years ago.

A man on Lowestoft fish market is never sacked, he is "spragged". nor does he sign on. He is "bumped on". Most local people will know what is meant when a trawlerman says "the gallas got heft under the quay." but what does a salesman mean when he calls that he has a few "gay backs". "Gay backs" are mackerel -not many of those on Lowestoft fish market these days and other fish, too, have unusual and attractive names. "Slips tongues" for instance, are small soles and "tea leaves" are small plaice.

There have been attempts by the White Fish Authority to introduce a standard list of names for fish, but the fishermen prefer the old ones and the fish fryers have their own. The coley. sometimes known as the coalfish or green cod. is a most attractive fish, but it does not command a very ready sale and is used chiefly for fish cakes and other processed foods. In London fish and chip shops it turns up as saithe. Dogfish has a long list of pseudonyms usually turning up in fish and chip shops as rock salmon, flake or huss. But so far no one seems to have come up with a new name for the lumpsucker, perhaps the most unlovely name of any fish!

Fortunately, our fishing fleet does not have very large quantities of oddly-named fish to dispose of. Its catch is largely prime plaice and soles for which it is justly famous throughout the country. The best Dover soles in the world, it is claimed, are landed at Lowestoft and for all the knack with names the fishermen have been unable to change the name Dover Sole to Lowestoft Sole. Another indication of the way in which names stick!

THE ERA OF SAIL

The pattern of fishing techniques has changed rapidly and dramatically since Lowestoft first began to emerge as a major centre following the construction of the harbour in 1832. In those early days Lowestoft, like the neighbouring town of Yarmouth, relied heavily upon the autumn herring voyage, when immense shoals of fish made their annual appearance on the traditional grounds and drifters put out to reap a harvest which seemed as if it would be repeated each year indefinitely.

There were two, less important voyages for the drifters earlier in the year, but the season which began in September was by far the most significant. At the start of this voyage the owners of fishing vessels gave a supper to their crews. The occasion was known as a bending-foy, a name derived from the first bending on of the sails, and a traditional ceremony was to fill and drain a punch bowl in drinking success to the voyage. When the Lowestoft china factory was in being towards the latter part of the 18th and early 19th century, some of the best china bowls produced were specially commissioned for these suppers, and were carefully preserved from year to year.

For hundreds of years before the building of the harbour, herring had been of major importance to the prosperity of the country. It was true that many of the early developments in catching methods were evolved by rival fishermen from Holland, but there could be no disputing the enterprise of the Suffolk men who, by the 15th century, were sending frail sailing boats to the distant northern waters from centres like Dunwich and Southwold to engage in line fishing for cod.

Somewhat primitive trawling techniques were being exploited by some English fishermen even before the 16th century, but major expansion and exploration of new grounds had to await the rapid improvement in communications which followed the Napoleonic wars.

Historically, therefore, the building of Lowestoft harbour was well-timed to secure the maximum advantage from an exciting period in the history of fishing in the North Sea. And this was even more the case with the development of the great railway network with its facilities for moving large quantities of fish quickly and efficiently from the ports to the big centres of population.

Visiting smacks from Ramsgate helped provide the necessary impetus when they began to use Lowestoft harbour a few years after its completion, and within a short time the modest beginnings of a local fleet had been established. Many of the local fishing luggers of the period were used for both trawling and drifting, and as the century progressed local experience gradually brought refinements of both sail and hull design.

Well before the 1880's Lowestoft had become a fishing port of considerable importance. Local drifters and trawlers, many of them built at the port, were designed to meet and overcome the harsh conditions encountered on the North Sea grounds. They were graceful and they were fast, and the men who sailed in them gained an enviable reputation for seamanship and skill.

Nearly all the vessels in the local fleet were clinker built, but in 1876 the local Richards yard turned out the 52-ft. fishing dandy *Nil Desperandum,* a carvel built drifter which was the forerunner of many similar vessels built at the port. A drifter of this type would be completed, ready for sea for as little as £360, and even allowing for the vastly increased purchasing power of the pound in those days the craft were clearly considered to be good value for money.

One vessel in this mould which passed into local legend *was* the drifter *Paradox,* built by Richards in 1884 for Walter Haylett, of Caister, and a craft which was reckoned to be able to leave most other sailing ships of her size well astern in any race.

By 1898 there were nearly 500 fishing vessels registered at Lowestoft, half of them sailing drifters and the rest sailing trawlers. Each autumn the local fleet was joined by the rakish visitors from Scottish waters, fifies and zulus with their dark brown and black sails complementing the red and tan of the canvas worn by the local fleet.

What was life like for the Lowestoft fishermen in those latter years of the 19th century, when it seemed both to them and to the proud local owners that nothing could ever displace the sailing craft which had been perfected by long experience?

Out on the fishing grounds of the North Sea there was little that was picturesque about fighting for survival in the teeth of a raging gale, even on board the sturdiest of smacks. Casualties among ships and men occurred with grim regularity. Many vessels came to grief within sight of home, when the tricky approach to harbour in bad weather could defeat the most skilful of skippers, and the beaches and inshore sandbanks claimed many victims.

There were other hazards, too, facing the fishermen. The notorious Dutch copers, or grog ships, were invariably in evidence on the grounds where the fishing fleets assembled, and talk of the evils of drink had a very real meaning when the liquor supplied was the vicious aniseed brandy served up by the copers.

The evils of the copers were finally overcome through the magnificent efforts of the Mission to Deep Sea Fishermen. It was the Mission which determined to meet the needs of the fishermen by taking out to the grounds well equipped ships able to supply not only cheap tobacco (which was a powerful inducement for men to visit the copers), but also sorely needed medical attention.

Before the arrival of the Mission ships in the early 1880's there was little which could be done for the fisherman unfortunate enough to suffer injury and injuries were caused all too often in the course of such hazardous operations as that of taking fish by small boat to be transferred to a fast carrier vessel.

Neglect and exposure caused terrible suffering at times. There was the case of a smack hauling in bad weather on the Silver Pits and which was struck by a heavy sea just as the beam trawl had been got on board but not secured. The force of the water swept the gear back into the sea, smashing the skipper's leg as it went. The accident happened on a Tuesday, and for three days after that the smack rode out a gale while the skipper had to fend for himself in the cabin until his injured leg could be lashed to the side of a fish trunk. Then, on the Saturday, he was transferred to a steamer, and not until the Sunday evening was he ashore and receiving expert attention. Another man who fractured a thigh remained untreated for nine days aboard a smack before he could be got back to port.

Looking back to his boy hood, a fisherman of the time recalled that for the first five years of his seagoing experience as an apprentice on board a sailing smack he never knew what it was to have a proper berth. He was expected to doss down on an old piece of netting in the fo'csle and to do without such amenities as heating or a change of clothing.

Another man. also at sea during much of Queen Victoria's long reign, looked back to his own apprenticeship on board a fishing vessel when "the time was spent at sea in lying, swearing, card-playing, fighting, sing-songing and telling ghost tales and stories about witches, which they for the most part were believers in".

The following extract from an article in the *East Anglian Daily Times* of April 11, 1887, gives a good impression of what living conditions entailed for hundreds of smacksmen when they came off duty.

"It is frequently past noon before the morning's catch is disposed of, and the weary hands are glad enough to go below to get their breakfast, throw off their oilskins, and perhaps their sea-boots and turn into their bunks. But there is little comfort in the cabin of a smack. It is a badly lighted, unventilated hole, about eight feet long and four or five feet high. The temperature is unpleasantly hot, generally between seventy and eighty degrees. The atmosphere is stifling. The smoke of strong tobacco and the fumes of cooking combine with the reek of damp oilskins and jerseys and a hundred other evil odours.

"The landsmen, stifled and nauseated, is soon driven to take refuge from suffocation on deck, and to face again the driving spray and the bitter wind".

Hard though conditions were on the old drifters and smacks, there were times when happier moments came along. Pride in the abilities of local craft and their crews, for example, led to the establishment of a whole series of races off the Suffolk port, when the pick of the fleet by a competed in thrilling contests which were often decided only by a matter of seconds.

During the regatta of 1882, vessels from Yarmouth were invited to race against the Lowestoft smacks, but they declined the challenge and on the day the event took place there were no contenders from the Norfolk port. This roused the Lowestoft men to be represented at the Yarmouth smack races held a little later and they returned triumphant when the local smack *Perseus* duly crossed the line in first place.

In the following year the Yarmouth men did race off Lowestoft, but to no avail. They came up against the crack skipper Jerry Crews, who won 13 out of the 14 races in which he commanded a whole series of smacks. In 1883 he triumphed at the helm of the *Gem* of *the Ocean.*

Pride in the local fishing vessels by the men who sailed them was matched by the builders, who never spared themselves to supply what was required. On September 1, 1897, for instance, an almost new local drifter, the *Breadwinner,* owned by George Catchpole of Kessingland, was wrecked on the North Beach at Lowestoft when returning to harbour to re-fit for the autumn herring voyage. On September 4 an order was put in by Mr. Catchpole at the local Reynolds shipyard for a new drifter. A keel had just been laid, and a month later the new *Breadwinner* was launched, in time to take the place of her predecessor on the herring grounds.

That year of 1897 was a significant one for Lowestoft for it was the year when another revolution in fishing methods began at the port with the launching of the wooden steam drifter *Consolation,* built by Chambers and Colby. An immediate success, the *Consolation* was followed two years later by *Test* and *Adventure,* which were also built locally, at the Richards yard.

By 1903 there were 101 steam drifters at Lowestoft, continuing a chain of events which had been inevitable since a steam capstan was first employed on a local vessel in 1884. The change to steam came with startling speed, especially at the Humber ports, but at Lowestoft many local trawler owners were reluctant to turn away from the sailing craft which had served the port so well. Indeed, many smacks returned to the Suffolk port after being replaced by steam trawlers at Hull.

Some of the best of the smacks were reckoned to be able to touch 12 knots under favourable conditions, and skippers were proud to match their craft against sail or steam on the way to the fishing grounds or racing back to port to catch the best markets.

As things turned out, Lowestoft was one of last strongholds of sail, and though over 150 local sailing vessels were lost in one mishap or another during a period of some thirty years before the first world war, many of the losses were made good in local yards which could build a smack in a matter of three months and have it fitted out ready for sea in a further fortnight

The sailing drifter had been virtually replaced by steam at Lowestoft by 1914, but in that year there were well over 250 trawling smacks working from the port.

Enemy action brought heavy losses to the Lowestoft sailing smacks during the 1914-18 war. and many fine vessels were sent to the bottom by German submarines after the fishermen had first been ordered to take to their small boats. During the four years of war over 100 smacks were destroyed, and when peace returned the Lowestoft sailing fleet had been reduced to some 180 vessels.

During the next year or so there was a last bid to recapture the glories of the past, and a handful of new smacks were built for optimistic owners. But it was too late. The sailing fleet s of continued to dwindle through the long and difficult years of economic depression and by 1938 only a score of smacks remained. In the following year just eight were still working from the port but then came another war and with it the end of an extraordinary era.

A few survivors were converted to motor power, and others were sold to Scandinavia where, remarkably, a number still survive under sail. Among these proud relics of an outstanding period is the Lowestoft smack *Diligence,* which was built at Brixham and joined the Suffolk fleet in July, 1893. The smack fished from Lowestoft until 1912, when she was sold to Swedish buyers as a coaster. In 1940 she was fitted with an engine, and there her story might have ended but for the remarkable enthusiasm of four young Swedish students. In 1965 these students bought the *Diligence.* restored her original rig and were so delighted with her performance that in 1969 they sailed her back across the North Sea for a nostalgic visit to her former home port.

They certainly built ships to last in the days when the *Diligence* first took to the water but Lowestoft has moved on apace since the time when hundreds of such sailing smacks jostled for space alongside the fish quays.

Even the proud age of steam has finally served its purpose and the last of the steam drifters, *Lizzie West,* was scrapped in 1961. The herring shoals have gone, perhaps for ever, and Lowestoft has now joined Yarmouth in having not a single drifter still at work.

Fishermen sail from Lowestoft today on board large, modern diesel trawlers equipped with every technical aid and designed for maximum efficiency and comfort. But the job of catching fish remains what it has always been a tough, demanding way of life calling for both skill and courage and with a heavy price to pay if vigilance is relaxed. The present generation of Lowestoft fishermen has provided worthy successors to that hardy breed of men who followed the same calling in the days when sail was supreme.

TAKING THE CURE!

In these days of radio, powerful lifeboats and helicopters, the plight of a fisherman taken ill at sea is hardly more serious than if he were safely ashore. A call by the skipper over the radio and the sick man is quickly on his way to hospital ashore.

It was very different in the days of the sailing smacks when the crew were cut off from all contact with the rest of the world and had to rely on the medical skill of the skipper and their own homely recipes. A fisherman with a broken arm, or even more serious injuries might spend days of agony before the vessel at last reached port and he was able to receive proper treatment.

But, injuries apart, the ailments of the smacksmen were little different from those of the present day fishermen. Saltwater boils, cracked hands, rheumatism and bronchitis are still the bane of the fisherman's life, to which, in recent years, must be added the infamous "Dogger Bank Itch" which has forced many a fisherman to come ashore permanently.

In the days when they had to rely on their own rough and ready resources, most fishermen thrust a bottle of their own favourite nostrum into the "oily" bag when they set off to join their ship. One old fisherman, for instance, always packed in his sea bag a couple of bottles of the liniment which had served him well when he had a badly bruised arm and it was freely available to all sufferers, no matter what their complaint!

On one occasion another Lowestoft smack sent word across that they had a member of their crew who was seriously ill with what they diagnosed as "brownkitis". After a brief conference, it was decided that "the liniment" might be effective in dealing with bronchitis and a bottle of the smacksman's cure-all was sent over by small boat. The liniment was plainly labelled "For external use only" but either the fishermen could not read or decided that desperate ills required desperate remedies! Regularly every two hours the sufferer from "brownkitis" was dosed with a gravy spoon full of the liniment. Soon he had finished one bottle and there was talk of sending across for the second one, but the skipper decided that they would wait a little while for the strength to come back to the patient. He was not disappointed! By next day the victim was back at work on deck.

The news of the cure soon spread through the fleet and few vessels put to sea without a bottle of the "physic". The local chemist who made up this wonderful cure continued to emphasise the fact that it was for external use, explaining that it was to be rubbed on the skin, and was not on any account to be drunk. But he knew full well that the fishermen ignored his warning consoling himself with the thought that even if it was taken internally it would take more than strong turpentine to kill a North Sea smacksman!

And to this day a liking for strong liniments still exists among the fishermen though it is doubtful if any of them risk drinking it. A local chemist still stocks a powerful liniment which, the label warns, is for "Cattle only". "The fishermen buy a lot of it," he explained. "They swear by it for sprains and rheumatics "screw-matics" as they call it. I tell them that it is only for cattle, but they laugh and say they've got hides tougher than an elephant. "But don't you try it, sir." he added hastily, "it'll have the skin clean off you!"

The "screwmatics" were, of course, the bane of the smacks-men. Constantly wet with little opportunity to dry their clothes, few escaped the twinges which came with increasing age, and many were crippled by it. Lumbago, too, was one of their chronic ailments. Eelskin garters were regarded by many fishermen as having almost a magical power in warding off rheumatism and lumbago. As the name implies, the garters were made from the skin of an eel and throughout the voyage were worn just below the knee. Men who suffered from lumbago often wore a belt made from eelskins. Another dodge was to carry a potato in the trouser pocket and many a fisherman claimed that his immunity from the "screwmatics" came from the wizen spud which he carried with him. When, despite his eelskin garters and potato, the fisherman was struck down by lumbago or rheumatism, his first action was to take down the bottle of liniment, possibly ending up his massage with a reviving slug from the bottle.

Then came the hot iron and the brown paper. An iron would be heated in the galley and. after the aching back had been insulated with layers of brown paper, a fellow member of the crew would start to "iron out" the pain - - while the patient prayed that the cook had not been over-enthusiastic in heating the iron and that his back was well-covered with brown paper! For those whose pain was not so great, or who feared the iron, there was the hot salt bag. The salt would be heated on a shovel in the galley and then poured into an old sock and then applied to the aching back.

The hot salt bag was also used for toothache, though some fishermen swore by a piece of sealskin which was gently rubbed on the aching jaw. A more violent remedy for toothache, where the molar was much decayed, was to thrust a red-hot needle into the cavity to "burn out the nerve"! In such circumstances the toothache usually disappeared before the final remedy could be applied! Earache was also treated with a bag of hot salt, but another remedy was the kernel of a boiled onion, inserted into the ear while still warm. Once again the temperature at which this was done called for delicate decision if the patient was not to go berserk at the ministrations of his "nurses"!

One of the most pleasant ways of dealing with toothache and certainly a simple one was to persevere in taking the left sock off before the right. If this was done at all times, it was said, the wearer would never suffer the slightest twinge! One doubts if it was very effective any more than curing toothache by cutting one's nails on a Friday, another cure! But undoubtedly the most popular cure for toothache was to immerse the offending molar in a mouthful of rum. Eventually the sufferer was quite unconscious of the pain and oblivious to practically everything else!

There was a similar "cure" for lumbago, a "long drink" being very much recommended. Judging by the number of pubs which used to cater for the fishermen, there was a lot of lumbago and toothache about! Norway Beer, sometimes called Black Beer, was also drunk as a cure for lumbago. Taken hot. or mulled by having a red hot poker thrust into it, it was a very popular beverage even when not taken medicinally. A number of Lowestoft off-licences still keep a small stock of Black Beer, occasionally sold under the name of Spruce Beer, and it is largely sold to old fishermen who don't believe in "'these modern concoctions".

Lowestoft fishermen, like many people, seemed to have more faith in something which came from overseas. They had a great admiration for the Dutch, both as seamen and as experts in sea-defence, but, above all the old smacksmen swore by Dutch Drops. A potent, evil-tasting elixir, Dutch Drops were taken for a vast variety of ills, but chiefly for the fishermen's curse, lumbago. They could be bought in Lowestoft, but this locally procured supply never had quite the same popularity as a bottle of the "gen-u-ine" stuff brought over from Holland. Any fisherman whose boat put into Ymuiden or one of the other Dutch ports was likely to return with a bottle or two for himself and his mates.

In at least one Lowestoft household a bottle of Dutch Drops, bearing an upright dagger surrounded by five star-shaped designs the coat of arms of Haarlem is still treasured. The instructions are to take five drops on a lump of sugar. Those who have tried the recipe recently say that it tastes vile according to old people the mark of a good medicine. The worse it tastes the more good it will do you, seems to be their motto.

So popular were the Dutch Drops at one time that a travelling salesman used to make a living out of hawking the little bottles round Lowestoft fish market. Even before the war, salesmen were to be found "barking" the Dutch Drops on market days, demonstrating with a wealth of dramatic talent how one dose transformed them from pain-racked wheezing invalids to hearty, upright men with voices like foghorns. But today, apart from a few relics in private medicine chests, Dutch Drops are forgotten.

Salt-water boils and hands chapped and cracked by long immersion in water have always been among the occupational hazards of fishermen. An old lady named Mrs. Love had a good name among the fishermen when it came to dealing with such sores. At her home in Denmark Road, not far from the harbour, she made up a simple ointment which soon became famous. "It was the most effective cure I have ever known for healing sea-hands hands which had been split by constant handling of wet ropes" was the testimonial of one old smacksman. It was also reputed to be extremely good for poisoned hands and stings. Universally known as "Mrs. Love's Ointment", it was one of the great panaceas of its day. With a bottle of Dutch Drops and a good supply of cattle liniment, the smack medicine chest was almost complete!

While most smacksmen preferred to rely on their own remedies. one or two of the vessels did carry a small medicine chest and a book of instructions. When a man was taken ill all the skipper had to do was look up his symptoms in his book. This would give the nature of the complaint and instructions as to which bottle he was to be dosed with. Each bottle bore a number and it was hard luck if your number was empty. One skipper, however, soon got round this difficulty. If the book said "dose with number nine" and there was no number nine left he merely gave half and half from bottles six and three! And no one seemed the worse for his arithmetical medicine!

Of all the ailments which beset the fishermen, however, possibly the worst feared apart from serious injury was the sting of the weever fish. Generations of fishermen have learned to treat it with the greatest respect, and with good reason. Modern research has shown that the sting of the weever contains a venom which is one of the most powerful pain-producing substances known to man. The weever carries its sting in spines which obtrude from its dorsal fin and above its gills, and over the years scientists have tried to find an antidote for its crippling venom which has been known to cause death.

A man who did a great deal of work on the weever venoms between the wars was the late Dr. H. Muir Evans of Lowestoft. A general practitioner in the town and honorary surgeon to the local hospital, he treated a great many fishermen for the stings of the weever. As a result of his experience and research, he became the leading authority on the subject. In a paper to the Royal Society, he described the effects of a weever sting and said he had known it to cause the death of a fisherman. The pain from the sting was so intense, said Dr. Evans, that he had known men try to hurl themselves overboard to end their lives and their agony.

It was in the late 1890's that Dr. Evans began his study of poisonous fish stings a study which he continued throughout his life. His interest began when the skipper of a Lowestoft smack was stung on the hand while clearing the nets off Cromer. It was a long beat home for the smack and by the time she reached port the skipper was in a critical condition. Despite all that Dr. Evans could do for his patient, he died. "This episode produced a profound impression on me," wrote Dr. Evans, "and I determined to investigate the nature and pathology of this new disease, and to find if possible a specific treatment for it".

It was an interest which extended to other types of venomous fish, and Dr. Evans even found a reference to the subject in the Bible. The 91st Psalm says: "There shall no evil befall thee that thou hurt not thy foot against a stone. Thou shalt go upon the lion and adder; the young lion and the dragon shalt thou tread under thy feet." Some of these references, claimed Dr. Evans, were to venomous fish which were well known to Hebrew fishermen.

One remedy advocated by the fishermen was to scorch the sting, while others wrapped it in vinegar and brown paper. The more desperate remedy was to hammer the sting with a belaying pin to numb the pain. Dr. Evans said that he had seen many maimed hands as a result. As a result of his research, Dr. Evans advocated injecting the sting with a five per cent solution of permanganate of potash. Kits, with a hypodermic and phials of the solution, were produced so that fishermen could give themselves an injection immediately on being stung,

More recently, in 1962. an American scientist, Dr. Findlay Russell, came to Lowestoft to carry out research into the weever venom. With the help of a local longshoreman, "Hurricane Hutch" Brown, he caught no fewer than 100 weevers in a single afternoon. Dr. Russell collected and analysed the weever venom, but the results of his work were a little disappointing as far as the fishermen were concerned. He confirmed that the venom contained a most powerful pain-producing substance. His advice was that the injections were of little benefit and that the fishermen should resort to the age-old custom of immersing the sting in warm water. This was just as effective as anything modern science could produce.

So another age-old cure has been justified *by* modern science. One wonders if there is anything in another one which is now being investigated by scientists. For centuries one particular variety of dogfish has been known to fishermen as the "nurse". They believed that when a fish was injured the "nurse" would rub itself against the wound and miraculously cure it! Now scientists believe that there may be something in the slimy covering of the "nurse" which does have a healing effect on wounds. It will not surprise the fishermen if it turns out to be true!

There are plenty of other old "cures" which might, just might, have a grain of truth in them. A herring a day, like the apple, is supposed to keep the doctor away, but its virtues as a medicine do not cease here. Far from it. Although one cannot get a herring or a pair of kippers under the National Health, they were highly thought of by physicians in the Middle Ages. The hard roe of the herring, beaten to a powder, was often prescribed for "the stone", while the flesh of the herring candied and dipped in honey was said to be good for asthma. The gills burned to a powder were highly regarded as a specific for epilepsy and a Dutch physician of the Middle Ages observed that a good herring eaten at the proper time supported the digestion. At no time, he remarked, did medical men have less to do than during the herring season when a great many of the fish were eaten. A herring eaten at night, said German doctors of the same period, relieved coughing, while the soft roe roasted with butter was said to be an excellent salve for frostbite. An elixir of herring bones was claimed to be good for the fever, as were poultices of salt herring applied to the soles of the patient's feet!

Nor were the virtues of herring confined to the human race. They were frequently used for ailments of cattle, a herring steeped in fat being said to be particularly good for the murrains. A Prussian farmer declared that he had saved his entire herd during an epidemic by feeding them a tarred herring each first thing in the morning. Just how he did it is not recorded!

The herring is certainly a wonderful fish and perhaps, despite their liniment and Dutch Drops, the old fishermen really had to thank the fish they caught, and ate in prodigious quantities, for their robust good health.

LIFEBOAT

As long as there have been boats and men in trouble in them, there has probably been some other seafarer ready to go out to their aid. The first life-boatmen probably paddled in a dug-out canoe! **But** if anywhere can claim to be the cradle of the lifeboat service as we know it today a team of men going out to save lives in a craft specially designed and built for the task it must surely be Lowestoft and district.

The history of the lifeboat at Lowestoft goes back nearly 170 years, to the year 1800 when Robert Sparrow, of Worlingham Hall, and the Reverend Francis Bowness, Rector of Gunton. Lowestoft. who were distressed by the loss of life in shipwrecks along the treacherous Norfolk and Suffolk coast, decided to raise a fund to build a lifeboat. The result was the inauguration of a lifeboat society and the money appears to have rolled in well. Most of the Suffolk villages contributed to the fund and it is interesting to find that Lloyd's Coffee House and Trinity House each contributed £30.

An appeal for funds which appeared in the *Ipswich Journal* in October 1800 declared:

"The first cost is £160 providing oars getting home, and building a boathouse will increase the expence to about 200 guineas a provision must be made for repairs; and though the seaman has hitherto shown his generosity by braving death in the horrors of a tempestuous ocean, with no other instigation than that of humanity, yet a generous public will see the policy and necessity of providing some additional regard, more particularly in securing a present supply to the families of those who are unhappily lost in the attempt."

And so the first lifeboat was built, by Greathead, of South Shields, at a cost of £160 and a new era of lifesaving should have begun.

THE BOLTON LIFEBOATS

The Bolton No. I Lifeboat with the Lifeboat shed -also the gift of Bolton- in the background.

Kessingland, and indeed many coastal towns and villages along the treacherous East Coast, can look back with pride on the selfless courage of its Lifeboat men, who saved many lives during the precarious days of sail. We are grateful too to those who provided the craft in which they put to sea. Some of these lifeboats were outright gifts from a single individual, others were the results of donations collected in many parts of the country.

In Kessingland it was the Beachmen themselves who, when they felt that a boat was needed, provided it themselves, buying the old Southwold lifeboat, the Solebay, in 1855 for £45, the RNLI contributing £10. She was in service until 1869. It was the people of an inland town, Bolton, who provided her replacement. Though far from the sea, Bolton had long been interested in such humanitarian work, supporting Manchester in raising money for the provision of lifeboats in various parts of the country. Over the years Manchester has provided no fewer than 17 Lifeboats.

Inspired by this record, the citizens of Bolton decided that now was the time to provide a lifeboat on its own. Towards the end of 1870 the committee announced that sufficient money had been raised to achieve this ambition and it was agreed that it should be handed over to the RNLI "For the purchase of a lifeboat to be stationed at Kessingland in the county of Suffolk and to be called *The Bolton*". The town of Bolton was agog with excitement about the new lifeboat and was so eager to see it that they made an official request that it should be transported to Bolton where it could be christened and exhibited. Manchester had held a similar gathering for a new lifeboat in 1864.

Unfortunately, the new Bolton lifeboat. which had been built at Great Yarmouth, was too large to be taken across country and the idea had to be abandoned. But Bolton did not go unrepresented at the handing-over ceremony on Kessingland Beach on Nov. 17th. 1870 Three members of the town's lifeboat committee had travelled overnight by train and had their first sight of the lifeboat. It was the first time they had actually seen a lifeboat! This Bolton was, as the village lifeboat-men had requested, of the Norfolk and Suffolk type, which was based on the old yawls which did such yeoman work along the coast. One thing very different from these yawls, however, was the use of seawater as ballast to stabilise the boat. Plugged holes in the hull enabled water to be let in when this practice was considered *a* safely factor. This 'flooding¹' of the craft was not very reassuring to landlubbers, but the Beachmen knew what they were doing. Speaking at the handing over ceremony, Kessingland's rector, Mr Crosse, said that the day marked the beginning of an interesting connection between the two communities, adding, "We have previously had some connection with the town because the furniture in the Church, the materials for the curtains and my surplices all came from Bolton - and they are all so good! Now this lifeboat! I think that the people of Bolton must be capital good fellows." The crowds on the Beach raised a cheer when it was announced that George 'Gaffer' Strowger had been appointed coxswain. He was to serve in this capacity for the whole of the service life of the Bolton.

Tragedy struck on July 17th. 1875, when the ketch *Mary's* was in trouble off Kessingland and, as the weather was too rough for a yawl to put to sea, the lifeboat was launched. It was while the boat was being put into the sea that one of the helpers got his leg caught in a coil of rope and was dragged into the sea. He was cut free, but at this moment a violent sea hit the Bolton and she capsized. Thirteen of the crew were thrown out and two others were trapped beneath the boat. Axes were used to smash a hole in the hull, one of the men being found and saved, but by the time the second man, Thomas Tripp was found, he was dead.

After over 22 years in service - during which she had been launched no fewer than 14 times, saving 47 lives, the Bolton was showing signs of strain and the Bolton Lifeboat committee decided they would start to raise money for a replacement. Collecting started in earnest with ladies being allocated areas for their rounds. They worked hard and long and were told that their labours would be rewarded by the naming of the new craft, 'The Ladies of Bolton'. But it was not to be! It was decided to call it 'The Bolton No. 2'

There was another disappointment too. Having had only a few representatives at the handing over of the first Bolton, the town had hoped that there might be a special excursion train laid on to the coast. But the railway company replied that this could not be guaranteed unless at least 200 tickets were bought. There were not enough bookings to meet this requirement - perhaps most people preferred to donate the money to collecting for more lifeboats! It was in June 1925 that the now ageing Bolton no. 2 went out of service, the Southwold Station having received a new motor-lifeboat. The redundant Bolton was eventually sold and converted into a houseboat. Between them, the two Boltons had given 55 years of service with *a* total of 54 launches during which they had saved 77 lives.

After all the strains and hazards of the sea, a more tranquil role as a houseboat must have been a welcome relief!

The Bolton No. 2 and its crew. I am grateful to Mr. Hans Boje of the Port of Lowestoft Research Society for these historic photographs.

KESSINGLAND LIFEBOATS

Freda Nathan, nee Strowger, has sent us a photograph of her Great Grandfather, George (Gaffer) Strowger, winner of two silver medals for lifeboat bravery. She also sent the excerpt from the book by Ernest Read Cooper,

Storm Warriors of the Suffolk Coast:

'Kessingland....appears to have had a Rocket Brigade in 1848 but no lifeboat. The Institution, however, placed two boats there in 1867, The Bolton and Lally of Broadoak: one of those boats was later on shifted about two miles south, to be opposite the most dangerous part of the Barnard and the Covehithe Channel, where vessels often came to grief in those days. She was locally known as the Benacre boat but was manned from Kessingland. This Benacre boat was removed in 1918 and I bought one of the boat-houses and had it removed to Southwold Harbour, where it stands on the quay a tribute to the good, solid work and stuff put into those places, before corrugated iron and the George V style came to defile the countryside. For a few years, from 1884 to 1896, there was a third lifeboat at Kessingland.

The most celebrated of the Kessingland coxswains was G. Strowger, known as Gaffer, who retired before 1911, after having earned the Silver Medal and Clasp for long service. Since the advent of motor boats at Lowestoft and Southwold, the need for one at Kessingland has passed. The station was finally closed in 1937 when the Hugh Taylor was removed. Ed. I. Smith (formerly of Southwold and well known as Young Barney) was then Coxswain and holder of the Silver medal; several others of the crew were in possession of the Institution bronze medal, first awarded in 1917 during the War. While this little record is being compiled (1937), comes the news that the encroaching sea has almost destroyed the empty lifeboat house, and that ex-coxswain Smith has also passed on.'

At the end of the book, the author notes the fact that in Canada, parts of the north shores of Lakes Ontario and Erie, showed places named after our coastal towns and villages, e.g. Yarmouth, Lowestoft, Covehithe, Southwold, Dunwich, Sizewell, Aldeburgh, Orford, Harwich and other East Coast places. Two of Freda's grandmother's sisters, Mrs. Strowger and Mrs. Farrow, both went from Suffolk around the 1830s, and settled at Guelph, near Toronto.

VILLAGE HEROES OF THE STORM

A century after she arrived on station in the village, a Kessingland lifeboat, which was later to achieve fame for a dramatic and daring rescue, is still in existence. She is the St Paul which is now in the RNLI museum at the former Royal Naval Dockyard at Chatham where they take pride in the fact that she is the oldest lifeboat in their collection.

Although one hundred years have taken their toll on her, there are plans to restore the St Paul to her former glory. The museum authorities tell me that work is soon to start, in this her centenary year, on long term full restoration.

St Paul, the gift of a blind doctor, James Paul of Barnes, Surrey, arrived at Kessingland in 1897 and was allocated to the No. 2 station at Benacre. A 38 foot Norfolk and Suffolk lifeboat of 12 oars, she had been built that year at a cost of £530.

When the No. 2 station was closed in 1918 she was transferred to the main station at Kessingland Beach and was housed in the existing lifeboat house, remaining there until 1931.

The rescue which brought her fame and honour came the following year, 1919, when the Rye sailing smack AJW was driven onto the Newcombe sands by a strong easterly gale and began to break up.

Tales of that wild night have been handed down from one generation to another. Gordon Hart still recalls his grandfather's account of the rescue.

"I was 14 years old when he died, but I still remember his tales of the sea, both as a fisherman and a member of the lifeboat crew," he told me, "Imagine what it was like getting a sailing lifeboat off the beach in that weather, freezing and with heavy snow squalls." He went on, "When the rockets were fired most of the Beach Village would turn out to give a hand in the launch. I remember my Grandfather telling me how he was trying to get dressed while running down the road!"

When the crew had assembled Coxswain George Knights discovered that he was two men short and called for volunteers.

"Two young lads stepped forward," said Mr Hart, "But they had never been to sea before!" The two missing crewmen, it transpired, were away at sea fishing, so the volunteers had to go! They were brave and willing, but they hadn't any experience and there was a near disaster off the Red House when the boat needed to go on the other tack. The lads just didn't know what to do." However when the St Paul was finally under control, it headed out for the wreck.

In a wild and severe storm, with men clinging to the rigging of the smack, Coxswain George Knights took a desperate chance. He drove the St Paul right over the submerged smack and snatched the crew to safety.

The heroism of the rescue was recognised by the RNLI, silver medals being awarded to Coxswain Knights and second Coxswain Edward Smith with bronze medals for the other lifeboat men for 'Their intrepid conduct.'

The saga of the St Paul is just one historic incident in the story of our lifeboats showing the courage of those who manned the lifeboats weeks ago and attributed tlo coxswain George Knights.

Harry Smith won his medal when he jumped overboard from the fishing boat Sarcpta, in heavy seas, to go to the aid of a fellow crew member, 22-year-old Alfred Marjoram. He reached the exhausted man and kept him afloat until they could be picked up.

His portrait was later painted on wood by artist Alan Davidson, "in admiration of his valour."

Kessingland School deputy head Gary Draper tells me that the portrait hangs today in the entrance to the school hall "and still follows the children with its eyes."

He adds: "We are very pleased and proud to retain this fine old picture."

Heroes all: Members of the crew of the Kessingland lifeboat St Paul. Those pictured included "Sandy" Hunter, "Turkey" Kemp, "Rue" Brown, H Thacker, A Wigg, L Smith, W Wigg, R Catchpole, "Doff" Muttitt, A Utting, H Hart, "Tubby" Knights, E Woolfield (secretary), E Smith and J Jeffries.

THE FOURTH KESSINGLAND LIFEBOAT

Having to go to Kent to launch the new books on Kent Village Signs, I decided it would be a good chance to visit Chatham Dockyard, where I understood the boat was restored and exhibited.

In spite of being from a nautical family, I did secretly wonder what *I* would do all day, after I had taken photographs of the boat for the second part of the Kessingland history, (to follow on from 'Stone Age to Stage Coach'), knowing that my husband would be interested in all that was going on and there was so much to see.

We started off with the Wooden Walls presentation, in sound and pictures, being a reconstruction of the life of an apprentice carpenter, taking a job at the Dockyard when the old sailing war ship 'The Valiant' was being built. It showed the er, tons of manpower, tons of wood from acres of trees and engineering skill needed to build a ship in those far off days. The scenery, sound effects and atmosphere made the whole thing very realistic.

Next we went over to the Lifeboats area, where we found the St. Paul in a very sorry state, with holes and lack of paint. On asking why the lifeboat had not yet been restored, we were told that it was the oldest one at Chatham and they had been unable to discover original plans on how she was built. They are waiting and hoping to restore her authentically. I am wondering if there were plans. After all the first Charter of the Suffolk Humane Society was signed after a meeting in the King's Head, Kessingland, in 1806 , in the presence of Lord Rous, the first Earl of Stradbroke. This was the forerunner of the R.N.L.I. If this boat was a former fishing boat, or built on the design of other fishing boats, maybe it was built on skills passed down from father to son? Would there have been formal plans?

According to Peter Cherry it was Kessingland's fourth lifeboat, given by a blind doctor, James Paul, of Barnes, Surrey. Our first was the 40' Solebay, purchased from Southwold for £83. £73 had been raised by Kessingland beachmen themselves and the other £10 donated from the RNLI.. She was purchased in 1856 and made her first rescue the following year. Next came the two famous Bolton Lifeboats, given to us by the people of Bolton, Lancashire, and the St. Paul served from 1918-1931. She was followed by the Hugh Taylor, here until 1936 when the Lifeboat Station here closed. Now motorised, it was very much faster to get out from Lowestoft and Southwold.

Back in Chatham Dockyard, Norfolk and Suffolk boat-building was highlighted with the impressive sights of the Waveney Lifeboats, built at Brooke Marine, taking pride of place at the forefront of the Exhibition. Other notable examples of local lifeboats we recognised the

Lord Reith etc. Close by the St. Paul, an authentic model of a horse and cart showed how horsepower as well as manpower was used to haul the lifeboats out and in.

We then explored the rest of the Historic Dockyard, with acres of history and activity, encompassing the whole history of shipbuilding in its original setting, from the ropery, where the huge ropes were manufactured, to the forges, wheelwrights, mast makers, sail-makers, armoury manufacturers, engines and the rest. You could go over a submarine built at Chatham, or the *Ocelot*, the last warship to be constructed there. There were ample places to eat, rest, relax or participate in reality experiences. The most amazing of all was to sit in a sixteenth century garden, with all the old English cottage garden flowers behind the Dock Commissioners house, with the formal garden, in which he would entertain Admirals and the like, set out beside it. Old-fashioned fruit trees spread-eagled the mellow walls, herbs and flowers intermingled and scented the warm air and no-one would believe you were only yards from the vast river Medway.

The St. Paul looks a sorry sight today, but East Anglian shipbuilding and expertise were in full view and the whole day out was an eye-opener into the skill and bravery of the men who braved the sea in days before radar, telephones or computerised instruments were dreamed of. It is good to see the dockyard still used and bustling with business, as well as being a living Museum and memorial to the past. What I expected would to be of interest to me for half an hour, lasted from 11 am to 5pm and there was not enough time to see a quarter of it.

As for Kessingland's old lifeboat, the Museum helpers assured me that the search for plans was still going on and they hoped to restore it to its past strength and good looks before they were done. They are very proud that it is their oldest exhibit.

I had never thought about the name of Kessingland's former lifeboat until I saw her in Chatham dockyard, so old, so fragile, so basic amongst all the others, mostly engine powered, spruced up in their bright paint and much, much larger.

The exciting and graphic description of one of St. Paul's shipwreck experiences, so poignantly told in the book of the Acts of the Apostles, chapter 27, must surely have been in the minds of Kessingland folk when choosing the name, obviously taking the 'Paul' from the surname of the donor. He would be a saint in the eyes of the village too!

As in the days of St. Paul, before mechanisation, boats were very much the same, relying on the skill and experience of the lifeboat men. They literally went out, in ferocious storms, as lifeboats are not needed in calm waters, with faith and prayer, just as is recounted in the Biblical account, where 276 men were miraculously snatched from a watery grave. Those who visit Malta on holiday and see St. Paul's Bay, can envisage those men crashing in onto the shore and safety, on bits of wood and planks from the broken ship, totally exhausted, as we are told. I remember when I went a few years back, I read the Acts account, a little each night, just to soak up the atmosphere (as well as to test my long-ago school French, since the Gideon Bible in the hotel bedroom was in English, Maltese and French).

The brave men who manned Kessingland's early lifeboats would no doubt go out in faith and prayer, leaving their wives, after helping to push the boat out, to pray for their safe return. Those who did not return were mourned, their loved ones comforted and helped, especially by the folk at the Bethel, the Sailor's Society church. They would not have volunteered as lifeboat men, had they not put others before themselves, in true Christian tradition.

(If any reader knows if there were original plans for building the St. Paul, or if they still exist, please get in touch with us or Chatham Dockyard.) *Maureen Long, 2004, Kessingland Times*

FRIDAY KEABLE'S STORY

The age of sail, the era of iron men and wooden ships, is recalled in the memories of 'Friday' Keable who first went to sea at the age of six in 1882

"I was born in Kessingland, Suffolk, of humble parents, my mother being the daughter of a farm labourer and my father a share fisherman". So wrote George 'Friday' Keable when, having retired from sea, he sat down to write the story of his life 'Fifty Years Ashore and Afloat'

His autobiography which he never completed, though he started it in 1934 and lived for another 15 years, has never been published, but I am lucky enough to have a copy of the manuscript.

It is a story of hard times and determination, the age of iron men and wooden ships when lads would go to sea in the sailing smacks at the tender age of eight years - or even younger!

"Being a big boy for my age and the eldest of a family of nine" he writes. "I was allowed to leave the village school at the age of eight and a half years.

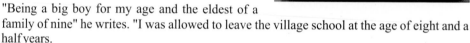

"Two years previously I had been taken to sea for what was called a 'pleasure trip', and well I remember it! It was in March 1882. the snow was on the ground and the weather bitterly cold. Not being in the mind for school that morning, my father gave me the option school or sea " I quickly made my choice, I can well remember the five mile walk to Lowestoft harbour with my father, I was wearing corduroy knickerbockers, wood-bottom clogs and an old jacket. My father towed me by the hand through the snow and slush and after about two hours trudging we arrived at Lowestoft harbour and went on board the herring lugger *'William and Alice'* of which my uncle was skipper and my father mate."

The 44 foot *William and Alice*, which had been built and was owned by Harvey Reynolds, carried a crew of ten hands.

"I was placed in the small boat which was lashed secure to the ship's rail" Friday goes on. "After an hour's sail from Lowestoft we lost sight of the land and I was very little interested in what happened on board the *William and Alice* from that time! But I do remember seeing the nets put out that evening at Sunset.

"I was very sick and bad at the time and wished I had gone to school instead: I should then have been home to tea having a round of bread and treacle and a mug of water out of the Hampshire well, and off to bed which was a very humble affair, but very much better than the bottom of a small boat, covered up with my father's old oily frock, and with his sou'wester turned inside out for me to be sick into!"

Young Friday had little appetite for food and sparse interest in his surroundings. By breakfast next morning, after the nets had been hauled, however, he had perked up sufficiently to try a fried herring and a ship's biscuit. "I can well remember eating the herring and biscuit and can recommend anyone suffering from seasickness to have a fried herring" he says, "It tastes just as good coming up as it does going down". With a gale blowing up the skipper decided to return to Lowestoft as the weather was too severe to continue fishing.

His homecoming was all he had dreamt of during two days of hard-lying at sea. "The old oil lamp was lit on the table and there was a home-made loaf and the treacle jar waiting for me. Mother fetched me some soft water from the old butt outside the door I had a good wash, my hair was combed, and I was placed near the fire with my bread and treacle. But instead of cold water I had a little

Lowestoft. Morning at the Quay.

Lowestoft morning at the Quay "depicts a scene which 'Friday' would have known well. It is postmarked "Lowestoft, 9.30am Feb 15. T909" and is addressed merely to "Mrs Spencer, Oulton Broad'. Hastily scrawled in pencil is the message: 'Am gone to sea in the Early Blossom " Obviously it was posted in complete confidence that it would be delivered the same day!

warm skimmed milk which was a special treat as I had been so seasick and had taken practically nothing to drink for two days

One would think that one trip to sea would have been sufficient to put a six-year-old off for life. But he adds "I was always ready for a trip to sea whenever I had the chance, and never asked about the size or condition of the boat, or the prospects of the weather!"

A couple of years later Friday went to sea full time on board the John Allen, owned by George Hunter, of Kessingland. His duties were to coil ropes and give a hand to the cabin boy who "was not man enough for the job".

Kessingland fishermen's part in the great herring voyage of the late 19th and early 20th centuries may have made the village 'the richest in England' but the money was hard-earned and there were times when money was short.

In his autobiography "Fifty Years Ashore and Afloat' Friday tells how. after that trip, he had to go back to the village school. He was back in the classroom for a couple of years, with breaks for the occasional trip to sea.

"When I reached the age of 12, being the eldest of the family and the biggest *boy* in the school, my father made application for me to leave and go to sea to coil ropes as cabin boy," he recalls.

He was allowed to leave on the grounds of hardship at home and the need for his financial help. "I was quite willing to leave and go to sea where I thought I should get a better living and be able to help my mother and the younger children" says Friday.

So the 12- year old Friday began his long career at sea, cabin boy and general dogsbody on the sailing boat *'John Allen'*, owned by George Hunter of Kessingland. His father was skipper and it was agreed that he would get no wages, but would receive a quarter of a share of the nett earnings.

"How well I remember our voyage! We left Lowestoft on July 16th, 1885 and our first port of call was North Shields. We fished from there for a week or two, then worked out of Scarborough and Grimsby till about September 29th".

The gross earnings for ten weeks at sea were around £140 and, after expenses had been deducted this left £70, which worked out at £4 10s a share. Friday received £1 2s 6d, plus three shillings 'Stockie' and his father's share was £6.

Then came the Home Voyage after which father and son received a total of £9 12s 6d.

"With that handsome sum we had a long cold winter to face with no income whatever and no prospect of being able to earn a shilling for at least three months, and the winters at that time were far more severe than we get in these days" he recalls.

"Well, our family managed to eke out through the long cold winter. Our chief diet was, for breakfast, bread and hot skimmed milk which we could get from the farm at three pints for a penny. For dinner, bread and a red herring with perhaps a slice of boiled swede which we could buy at 3 pence a bushel. On one, or perhaps two days a week we would have a treat. Mother would send me to the butcher's for a pennyworth of scraps which she made into a big scrap pudding about the size of a cork fendoff which was used on the old *'John Allen'*

"This was served hot with a slice of swede and turnip and was a real good dinner! For tea, more often than not, just a piece of bread and treacle and then off to bed, which was far better than sitting up late with very little or no fire".

He adds "I may tell you, I experienced more than one winter under very similar circumstances".

As a young man, after a hard apprenticeship in sail and rising to become skipper, 'Friday' Keable saw the first indications of a profound change in the herring fishing.

Steam arrived on the scene and the first man to have a steam drifter built at Lowestoft was a Kessingland man, George 'Mouse' Catchpole.

"About 1896" writes 'Friday' in his autobiography, "Mouse dissolved his existing partnership and launched out as a pioneer of the steam drifter. He had built to his order the very first steam drifter to be registered at the port of Lowestoft. She was called *'Consolation'* LT718. He skippered her himself for about two years.

After that he stayed ashore and became the owner and part-owner and manager of several new drifters. In the year 1901 he promoted a limited company, the *Star Drift Co.,* of which he was managing director and I was his Commodore Skipper."

It was in that same year that 'Friday' himself bought a steam drifter.

'I joined in partnership with one or two of my best friends and bought one of the very early steam drifters". The vessel was the *'Success'* LT161 which was then only six months old. One can guess that 'Mouse' Catchpole was one of the partners and the one who acted as manager.

One of the partners was another Kessingland man, Mr. Arthur Gouldby. "He called himself a sleeping partner, but I can assure you that it was only a nickname for him as he was always very wide awake! He was also greatly interested in the fish-buying branch of the business with controlling interests in many parts of the trade.

Writing in 1934 'Friday' adds: "in addition to all this he is a farmer with land and property all around him and has been for the past thirty years a very important man and a great support to the working population of his native village of Kessingland. He is one who would be greatly missed for the interest he has always taken and the great kindness shown to the poor of the village. May he be spared many years in health, happiness and prosperity."

Kessingland men were certainly a dominant force in the herring industry. Messrs. C. and R. Harvey, who were Kessingland born, were early in the field with the steam drifter *'Test'*.

The race for steam was on and one of the most successful builders was Sam Richards who developed his own engine works which were fitted with the first electric light in East Anglia!

Owners couldn't wait to buy a steam drifter and they 6, were coming off the launching ways at an amazing speed. But Sam Richards excelled himself when, in 1906, he built the *'Briton'* in 40 working days. She sailed straight out of harbour on the 40th day. Sam bought himself a motorcar, the first man in Lowestoft to own one.

It was a wave of prosperity which made Kessingland 'the richest village in England' and gained it the nickname 'Klondyke'.

The photograph shows one of these early steam drifters, the *'Request'*. With her tall Woodbine funnel she looks an odd craft, but she went on fishing until 1933!

KESSINGLAND CHARACTERS

People often complain that there are no 'characters' about today. The old village, they say, was full of them, but today we are a pretty dull generation. I still recall with delight the tales of these old characters. There was "Donks", for instance, who was so pleased with his new bike that he kept getting off to see how he looked on it!

Skipper 'Friday' Keable in his memories of old Kessingland yarn about "Donks" told how he sold his gun to buy ammunition for it. Then there was the time when he bought a new linen post and sawed it in half as it was too heavy to carry home.

Donk's father was a good old workman who was employed for £1 a week and a pint His employer always said his man thought more of the pint than he did of the £1 - the pound was for his wife, but the pint was for himself!

They were hard times when food was often short and no-one can blame them if they took full advantage of the occasions when it was plentiful. The driftermen had prodigious appetites for herring and a crew of ten would normally get rid of 70 for breakfast with plenty of bread and strong tea. But one Kessingland fisherman was such a glutton for them that he usually consumed 16 for breakfast - a feat which led the boy cook to complain to the skipper that he couldn't keep pace with him.

"Some years later" 'Friday' recalls, "this man worked on a farm. Wages were very low. Although living was much cheaper than it is today, his wife could not afford to supply him with sufficient of even the most common food. The farmer often heard complaints from the man on those grounds, so he decided that for once he would provide him with a dinner. He arranged with his wife to cook 'Lossie' a dinner which she felt was a reasonable quantity for six men! The dinner was taken out to him in the fields in a wheelbarrow, together with two pints of beer. Lossie cleared the lot and told the farmer's wife that it was a splendid dinner and he would like one again tomorrow!"

Lossie may have been a great herring eater, but he fell far short of being champion. That title would seem to go to Amos Beamish, the Giant who has claimed that on one occasion he ate 30 herring at one sitting at a special event. He had been challenged to a contest by 'Lion' Kerrison, a Yarmouth drifterman. 'Lion' downed 29 herrring, cried 'enuff and Amos clinched it with a total of 30 He added insults, remarking that he wouldn't mind another half dozen.

There was little talk of slimming in those days when people were striving to find enough to eat. They made the most of what was plentiful.

SCHOOLS

Kessingland children have passed through the upper school in Church Road since it opened in 1869 No doubt this old photograph of one group will bring back memories. Do you recognise anyone? Can anyone say when it was taken?

Soon. I suppose, most of the old buildings will disappear, including the first schoolroom which was opened over 120 years ago. A hotchpotch of buildings grew up on the site over the next century, but it could not keep pace with the growth of the village and finally, in 1986, the move was made to the new school in Field Lane,

just how schooling has changed since those early days was demonstrated when the then headmaster, Terry Weatherly staged an exhibition to mark the end of an era with the building of the new school.

One of the most interesting and valuable exhibits was the school logbook which went back to that opening in 1869 when there was a total of just 55 pupils.

Schooling in the Victorian age, it is apparent from the logbook, was more strict but, at the same time more free and easy.

There seems to have been a never-ending series of excuses for dodging off school. A wreck on the beach was always an excuse for the lads to disappear. At other times they claimed to be helping father with his nets. The girls were always ready to skive off to look after the babe while mother worked in the fields.

Holidays were also allowed for such events as Royal betrothals, weddings, village 'treats' and even 'amusements' at the King's Head.

There were periodic campaigns to clamp down on truancy. One headmaster wrote "A great many children idling about the parish who ought to be in school". This was followed by a purge and it is recorded that the truants were 'severely punished'.

Discipline suffered towards the end of the last century when fishermen were allowed to attend classes. They had to swot up on their reading and writing so that they could take the Board of Trade exams for their mates' or skippers' tickets'.

The school logbooks record these fishermen schoolboys as 'noisy' and 'disorderly'. It is said that when lessons got a bit of a bore they were not adverse to lighting up their clay pipes or nipping across to the King's Head for a pint!

The periodic epidemics which swept the village measles, scarlet fever, chickenpox and whooping cough also affected attendances. So did chilblains which were the bane of children's lives in an age when there was little in the way of heating and some had no shoes.

One of the most tragic entries in the logbook comes on July 16th 1875: "Beach children absent on account of the terrible calamity which happened last night, the stranding and upsetting of the lifeboat in an attempt to reach a vessel in distress on the Barnard Sand",

"One of the crew, Tom Tripp, was crushed to death by the boat falling on him. All the others of the crew more or less hurt".

Life with all its tragedies, mishaps and ill health never seemed to have run smoothly in Victorian Kessingland.

It must have been with some relief that one headmaster was able to record: "Nothing unusual happened today".

HARD CHEESE FOR SAILORS AND PAUPERS

It is clear from the Overseers' accounts that bread. cheese, milk and porridge formed the staple diet of the poor of Kessingland during the 17th and 18th centuries. They had other foods, too, including butter from time to time, but cheese at around tuppence a pound was always a good standby. Undoubtedly both the butter and cheese were local products and they had a high reputation. In Elizabethan times the historian Camden declared that great value was set on Suffolk Cheese "which is vended in all parts of England - nay, Germany. France and Spain". Suffolk butler was also highly renowned, but while its reputation soared, that of our cheese declined. The two were not unconnected. Increased production of butter meant that more milk was skimmed to provide the cream for its making. The milk was skimmed twice and sometimes even three limes, leaving a whey so thin it was known as 'sky blue'.

It was this skimmed milk which was largely used for the cheese - a product which was known as 'Suffolk Bang' and which became a laughing stock throughout the country.

There were all sorts of jokes and sarcastic remarks about our cheese.

"Pigs grunt at it; dogs bark at it, but none bite it" was one sneering description. Some people claimed to have made door latches out of the stuff - latches so strong and durable that they outlasted the wooden ones! Then there were those who swore by it for wheelbarrows. That flat, circular cheese, they said, made a wonderful wheel. In addition to being durable, it had a slight resilience which absorbed some of the bumps!

Of course, there were some good Suffolk cheeses to be had, but one had to find a farmer who did not churn butter - and they were a rarity.

By the 18th century it was regarded as remarkably bad. Defoe, in his travels through the Eastern Counties, remarked that Suffolk produced possibly the best butter in the country - but certainly the worst cheese. Even the Suffolk poet Bloomfield could not find a good word for his native cheese:

"It, like the oaken shelf on which 'tis laid Defies the effort of the bending blade Or in the hog trough lies in perfect spite Too big to swallow and too hard to bite"

But despite Bloomfield's scathing rhyme, there were those who bought Suffolk cheese - and in large quantities. It was widely advertised as suitable for ship's stores. The Admiralty bought tons of it and other owners were good customers. There is the story of a ship which set out on the long voyage to India with a consignment of Suffolk cheeses in an ironbound chest. During the long voyage, rats gnawed their way into the chest, but on finding what it contained, fled without even a nibble!

That seems to be carrying a good story a little too far, but Suckling, in his 'History of the Antiquities of the County of Suffolk', gives his verdict: 'Suffolk cheese is proverbially execrable' he says. Of course makers of the cheese dismissed such sneers as a ploy to take their trade and it was all a joke which had gone too far. The final say seems to have been left to the Royal Navy. After the sailors had complained bitterly about Suffolk cheese -claiming that it was only fit for making buttons - the Victualling Board in 1758 looked into the matter. It was, they said 'cheap, thin, hard and durable, but practically inedible!' Orders for Suffolk cheese were cancelled and Cheshire or Gloucester - both more expensive - bought instead. It was a blow for Suffolk farmers who had been selling 1000 tons of it a year to the Navy alone.

Despite it all, our cheese seems to have survived for I find a Victorian cook book recommending it - as an ingredient for plastering walls! It was, apparently a Roman recipe for plaster - a mixture of sand, lime, grated cheese and hot water. The cook book suggested that those trying out this curious recipe should use Suffolk cheese. It was the final insult!

HEMP ANCIENT SITE NOW ALLOTMENTS

Looking down on what was the old Hemp Pit - now well-tended allotments in Whites Lane, Kessingland. In addition to hemp, the Pit was also used for soaking osiers for the village basket makers.

For centuries, going back to Saxon times, hemp was an important crop in Eastern England, providing fibres for the making of a range of products, including linen, nets and ropes. Like many other towns and villages in the region, Kessingland had its own Hemplands and the accounts contain many references to the harvesting and processing of the crop - entries such as 'Caning and laying the poor's hemp in the water and taking it out again and carrying it about'.

After harvesting, the stalks of the hemp had to be laid to soak for some weeks so that they could 'ret' or rot, after which they were beaten to release the fibres. These were then spun into yarn and used in weaving and in a variety of other ways.

It was an ancient craft going back to Saxon times when, it is known, they traditionally buried their dead in hempen cloth.

Kessingland's Hemp Pit still exists today as the site of the allotments in Whites Lane. They are several feet lower than the adjacent ground and since the springs that fed the pit still flows to some extent, the area is remarkably wet in winter. It has the advantage, however, that it retains more moisture in summer droughts.

So important was the production of hemp that both Henry VIII and Elizabeth I issued orders for the growing of the crop 'for the better provision of netes and the furtherance of fishing and for eschewing idleness'. There were fines on farmers who failed to fill their quota. Henry fixed it as 3s 4d, but Elizabeth tipped it to a punitive £5. This provoked such outrage in East Anglia that the Act was repealed in 1593.

When Charles II came to the throne he struck another blow to the hemp trade. To help the wool trade he ordered that all those buried should have a shroud of wool rather than the traditional hemp. Fines were imposed on families which failed to obey the law. though there were many who ignored it and followed tradition.

Among other uses hemp was used widely in the making of canvas - a name said to be derived from 'cannabis'. The growing of cannabis is, of course, illegal these days and I often wonder if a man so charged could plead in defence that he was merely obeying the laws of Henry and Elizabeth and that he hoped to sell his crop to the Royal Navy!

Kessingland's hemp was grown on the Heathlands to the north of the village, not far from the terrace known as The Oaklands'. For generations it was steeped in the Hemp Pit. or 'Mardle' as it was known. It is clearly marked on a map of 1783, but it was probably used for long after that date. Hemp was still being grown in parts of the country, early this century but just when Kessingland ceased production is not known.

Certainly it went on for hundreds of years and it has been suggested that the history of the site goes back to even earlier times. It was, it is claimed, probably a defensive site surrounded by banks and thorn hedges into which cattle could be herded - and in which women and children could take shelter - when the Danes and Saxons made their savage raids on the coast.

The same suggestion has been made in relation to Carlton Colville's former hemp pit which was partially filled in some thirty years ago. At times, it is thought, both these flooded areas were used for soaking and stripping of osiers. Certainly Kessingland had its basket makers who would have needed a plentiful supply of willow canes.

Much is unknown about the origin of the Hemp Pit and when it was finally taken over as arable land. One thing is certain, however. Those who tend their crops on the allotment are working on historic land.

THE SLUICE

For centuries ever since Kessingland harbour silted up the Sluice on Benacre Ness has been of prime importance to those who farm the reclaimed marshes drained by the River Hundred. For over 50 years the river has been discharged into the sea by powerful pumps, but before that the drainage was by gravity and a very troublesome business it was.

It was a relatively simple system but, like anything to do with the sea, it was fraught with difficulties. The tunnel was frequently blocked by sand and shingle and, with the beach building up. it had to be lengthened until it was nearly 200yards long.

It is all due to the slow movement north of Benacre Ness which results in the build-up of the beach to the north and erosion, such as is now taking place at Easton Bavants, to the south.

The northward movement of the Ness seems likely, in the future, to present problems for the pumping station which drains the marshes of the River Hundred.

Draining the Hundred to the sea has been a problem for centuries, ever since our ancient harbour silted up and the land was reclaimed and drained for farming.

Not a lot is known about the loss of our harbour some 400 years ago, or how and when the land was reclaimed. I have been lucky enough, however, to have come across a little booklet "The History of Benacre Sluice" which was written by John Oldrin before the last war. It was sold for sixpence, all the proceeds going to Lowestoft Hospital.

Farmer Oldrin lived within 500 yards of the Hundred for all his life The river, he explained, drained some 16,000 acres of land, all the water being discharged into the sea at Benacre Ness.

"I have learned": he wrote in his booklet, "that a great many years ago (some hundreds of years) the various owners of properties made arrangement to drain these lowlands. To do this they built a wooden trunk under the sand-cliffs and the beach to the edge of the sea, placing a door at the freshwater end. To let the water out this would have to be lifted up by manual labour twice every 24 hours and also let down".

At first the connecting trunk was a short one, but it had continually to be lengthened. Last century it was 100 feet long. The longer it became the more difficult it was to keep it clear of sand and shingle.

Many a time, recalled Farmer Oldrin, he had to drive his men a distance of five miles as early as five o'clock in the morning to clear the trunk. With the outlet to the sea blocked, the marshes and the main road would be flooded.

Work on building a new sluice was started in 1936. but was delayed by heavy rains and storms which flooded the marshes. Eventually it was completed and a new pumping plant was installed at a cost of over £13.000, but Mr Qldrin remained convinced that a properly designed gravitational system would have been equally efficient and cheaper. But that was before the 1953 floods which burst through at the sluice, destroyed the pumping station and flooded the marshes, cutting the main A12. A new pumping station was built and has operated satisfactorily since. But one never knows with the sea!

An old view of Kessingland beach looking south towards Benacre Ness

The last few years have seen remarkable changes in our beach. Today, where the waves once lapped the foot of the sea wall, we have a wide expanse of shingle even greater than the beach shown on this old photograph,

RATS

Kessingland High Street early in the 20th century, probably much the same as it was when, on Christmas Eve 1883 a 17-year-old seaman set out on a 12 mile walk from Lowestoft harbour to his home at Southwold. It was a hard trudge in the middle of the night and one which was to end in the horror of being pursued by hordes of rats. The story was told to me by 88-year-old Mr. C. Hurr, of Sudbury.

The man who escaped a horrible fate was his father Walter 'Barlow' Hurr. "Father was one of a family of 17 whose home was in Southwold". He told me. "Like most of his family he went to sea. a member of the crew of the ketch *Lucinda,* The Ketch berthed in Lowestoft late on Christmas Eve and the rest of the crew, which included three of his brothers, did not fancy a long walk home, so they booked in at the Mission". But young Walter, loaded with gifts, including smuggled tobacco and spirits, was eager to get home with his festive cheer

"At that time, in 1883. what is now the A12. was little more than a rough track, all mud and ruts" said Mr. Hurr, "but he hoped to make it home in about three hours. He was going well when he passed through a darkened Kessingland and it was not until he was striding alongside Benacre Park that he sensed something sinister behind him".

Walter's first fear was that the Revenue Men were on to him. As things turned out he would have been glad if it was only that. He hurried on into Wrentham, the hair prickling on the back of his neck as he sensed something fearful behind. It was getting closer! Stopping at South Cove Church, he looked back and saw, for the first time, what lay behind it was a vast horde of rats.

"Behind him the road had come alive. It was moving up and down, flowing towards him in a relentless tide" said Mr. Hurr In desperation he threw his carpet bag over the churchyard wall and scrambled after it. wedging himself into a niche between a buttress and the wall of the tower "From there he saw a vast and loathsome army of rats of all sizes led by a king-sized veteran."

The young seaman watched in terror as thousands upon thousands swarmed past, only a few

yards from his hiding place At last the road was clear, only a foul stench remaining as a reminder of their presence. It was a white-faced Walter who finally stumbled into his home in Southwold with a remarkable story to tell. Was he exaggerating? Had he had a little too much of his Christmas cheer?

His story was dramatically confirmed a few days later when a local newspaper published an account of how, that Christmas Eve, a large field of turnips near Potters Bridge had been destroyed by rats. In that field was found the body of a man who had been attacked by the rats' He was still alive and was taken to Bulcamp Workhouse, but he had been so viciously attacked that nothing could be done for him and he died on Christmas Day.

"From that day onward my father would never take that walk from Lowestoft alone or at night" Mr. Hurr concluded.

MORE RATS ...

More tales of rats have been coming in since my story about the young seaman who was terrified by a vast horde on the Lowestoft-Southwold Road towards the end of the last century.

One of the most remarkable is about the giant rat which, in 1939, blacked out 250 square miles around Lowestoft and Yarmouth!

As their homes were shaken by explosions and the night sky lit up with lurid flames, many people were convinced that war had come.

It was not war, but it was an alarming night. One man was killed and five were injured in explosions at the Yarmouth Power Station on the evening of March 20th 1939.

The first explosion came shortly after seven o'clock that evening when a transformer blew up and caught fire. Immediately Yarmouth and Lowestoft and much of the surrounding area were plunged into darkness. In Yarmouth itself, the explosion, plus the steam and smoke clouds over the power station, the green, white and blue flames and sparks convinced some people that the town had been bombed.

Getting a little panicky, people began to ask: "Has the war started?" Trial black-outs had been held earlier in the year, ARP volunteers were already training and everyone knew that war was coming. Was this it? ARP volunteers began to report in for duty and fears that the balloon had gone up were heightened by a second massive explosion and more vivid coloured lights in the sky.

Firemen arriving at the power station minutes after the first blast obviously feared a second one. They emerged from the building to warn the crowds "Run for your lives". Few needed a second warning!

The crowds scattered, but the firemen and police remained at their posts. A group ventured into the power station headed by a police chief inspector. Just as they did so, they were knocked down by a second blast. All escaped serious injury, though the inspector staggered out, his clothes a mass of flame.

A German bombing raid was soon ruled out as the cause of the explosions. But what had happened? It was only some time later that experts decided that the first explosion had been caused by a giant rat! It had scrambled on to one electrical terminal and then, somewhat incautiously, had stretched out its forepaws to span across to an adjoining one! The resulting short circuit of 6000 volts had incinerated the rat, and caused a massive explosion. It must have been a monster rat to make such a span, but it had devastating results, said the experts.

The short circuit had caused a transformer to blow up, setting fire to the bath of oil in which it was running. So fierce was the heat that copper, iron and lead were burning, giving vivid, ominous colours in the night sky.

The second explosion came when another transformer was switched in. This, too caught fire.

The black-out lasted about 90 minutes and though it was not caused by bombing, the incident provided a valuable rehearsal for what was to come when the air raids started. There was some panic on the streets, but most people carried on 'business as usual'. Shops sold out of candles, in the Regent Cinema the organist played by the light of a flickering gas jet and in Lowestoft town hall the finance committee continued its meeting by candlelight. For all they knew the Germans might have come but the show, and business, had to go on!

SMUGGLERS

Five and twenty ponies
Trotting through the dark
Brandy for the Parson,
'Baccy for the Clerk
Them that asks no questions isn't told a lie
Watch the wall my darling, while the Gentlemen go by!

For as long as there have been customs duties and taxes there have been 'Free Traders' - better known as smugglers - ready to turn a dishonest penny by evading them. The Romans introduced a range of taxes and restrictions on trade, but their historian Tacitus recorded that the Britons paid their taxes 'with cheerful readiness' . Down the centuries, as the taxes multiplied, they became less cheerful about the matter and there was a growing appreciation of the efforts of the smugglers to lighten the burden. In Tudor times the import taxes do not seem to have been particularly onerous, the range of goods including hops, bricks, barrel hoops and - would you believe it - onions! Things looked up in the 1710 century when excise duties were levied on spirits, beer, coffee, tea and cocoa as well as tobacco and, surprisingly, on sherbet! With these new taxes, the stage was set for the golden age of smuggling during which the empty beaches of Suffolk played an important role. Kessingland was among their favoured landing spots. In July 1746 it is recorded that a gang of 50 smugglers armed with cutlasses and firearms landed a cargo of tea and brandy on the beach at Benacre Warren, followed a fortnight later by two 'runs' of contraband - one to Benacre and the other to Kessingland Haven. The gang involved was so large and well armed that the Excise Officers, even with the help of the militia, could do nothing to stop them.

A few days later a party of upwards of 70 smugglers passed through Benacre Street with a huge cargo of contraband and, once again, no attempt was made to stop them. Once a contraband cargo was ashore the goods were swiftly moved inland, on their way to London, Ipswich and Norwich - and to local customers, many of whom seem to have been parsons: hence Kipling's rhyme 'Brandy for the Parson, 'Baccy for the Clerk'.

It is not surprising that local clergy of that era showed little hesitation in buying contraband since, in the 16th century, privileged members of the church hierarchy were allowed considerable duty free supplies of wine. Bishops were allowed over 3000 gallons a year; Deacons and Provosts 756 gallon.. All wine for the Royal Household was duty free. Naturally the local parson felt that he was entitled to some small indulgence

Best known of these clerical customers was Parson Woodforde of Weston Longville near Norwich. In his diary he frankly recorded his purchases of rum and gin delivered to him straight off the boat and adds 'Very busy this morning in bottling two tubs of gin and one of Cognac Brandy'.

But Parsons could sometimes be the dupes of smugglers rather than their customers. The story is told of how the Rector of Lowestoft, the Rev Francis Cunningham, was persuaded to carry out the burial service for a sailor who, he was told, had died on board a ship anchored off the port. The Rector was astonished to hear the next day that the grave in St Margaret's Churchyard had been opened and the coffin carried away. It transpired that Mr Cunningham had read the burial service over a coffin full of valuable lace which, by this time, was already on the London market

The end of the Napoleonic wars early in the 19th century saw a boom in smuggling which led to the formation of the Coastguard Service with lookout stations along our coasts. Kessingland was among those on this stretch of the coast. It was to keep watch for around half a century before the service was disbanded in 1923, its duties being taken over by the newly-formed Preventive Service. The photograph shows the Kessingland station around

the turn of the century with a rating, telescope at the ready, still scanning the sea for the smugglers.

Many an inn on this stretch of the Suffolk coast has a reputation for having been the haunt of smugglers. Perhaps the most famous, as well as the prettiest, is the Queen's Head at Blyford. The thatched inn stands just across the road from All Saint's Church and legend has it that a secret tunnel ran between the two. Then there are tales of a secret room in the Crown Inn at Snape; of kegs of gin under the Altar cloth at Theberton Church; and barrels of contraband hidden in the valley of the double roof of St Andrew's, Westhall.

The old-time smugglers were still plying their illicit trade well into the last century. In his 'Norfolk and Suffolk Coast', published some ninety years ago, W.A.Dutt says "Smuggling is by no means extinct in Lowestoft as far as the bringing in of tobacco and cigars and bottles of scent is concerned, but it is a petty business compared with what it was a century ago". There were men who could hark back to links with those days. One Lowestoft man told him that the last member of the 'old gang' was Mr James Saunders, who was known as the 'King of the Smugglers', kept a small inn in Kirkley (could it have been the Plough and Sail?).

"In his sixties, when his race was nearly run, he was a hale, burly bluff old fellow, over six feet in height, a little strident in voice, and with a manner commanding respect and ensuring obedience. His inn was the resort of many who loved to hear tales of the seafaring life and especially of the old 'free-trading' days." Looking back on them, those smuggling days - despite their violence - have a nostalgic appeal bound up, as they were, with the daring men in the days of sail- Today smuggling is still a vast trade, but the container lorries and Transit vans lack the romantic appeal of the fast lugger and the Revenue cutter.

Around the middle of the last century when a bitter war was fought against the smugglers, it seems extraordinary that fierce battles were fought and fortunes made by so innocuous a beverage as tea - though tobacco and brandy were also part of the smugglers' trade.

We no longer have a coastguard station at Kessingland, but the problem of smuggling is still a serious one. Today it is drugs and illegal immigrants which come ashore.

With only a short passage across the North Sea from the Continent, the Suffolk coast was a prime area for the smugglers. Covehithe, Benacre and Sizewell were among their favourite spots. The rivers, creeks and deserted beaches made it an ideal haunt.

It was the exorbitant tax on tea which made the fortunes of the smugglers and there was a ready market for the contraband. Even the clergy were not averse to a duty free cup of tea!

Most of the tea came from the Netherlands where Dutch traders bought it for around sixpence a pound. They sold it to the smugglers for two shillings. Once across the North Sea it fetched over six shillings a pound. Brandy, gin and other spirits also met a ready market. Gin was said to be so cheap that smugglers' wives used it to clean their windows, claiming that it gave the best finish. There's a tip for those who complain that they can't get rid of the smears.

There were also heavy taxes on such things as chocolate, salt, leather and soap, but there seems to have been little trade in these - no record of a smuggler being caught in possession of bars of soap! It is part of the legend of smuggling that the parson was frequently involved and that, very often, there was a tunnel from the church to the nearest inn, like The Queen's Head at Blyford.

Although they had their successes, the coastguards were far out-numbered by the smugglers and it is recorded that on one occasion the preventive men were present when an illicit cargo was landed on Kessingland beach, but were not in sufficient strength to intervene!

The bottom was knocked out of the market in the 1840s when the Government slashed taxes - one of the few occasions when a recession, at least for the smugglers, was caused by drastic cuts in taxes!

They were a violent and ruthless band of men, but how innocent the tea smugglers seem compared with those who, these days, trade in the evil of drugs,

BEATING SHEDS

When this old postcard appeared early this century Kessingland had a lot of beating sheds and net stores. While the men folk were away after the herring shoals their wives and daughters were busy mending the nets. And, considering that one drifter alone could shoot up to a mile of nets, and that they were easily torn and damaged, there was plenty of work for all. Those were the days when Kessingland was known as 'Klondyke' - the richest village in England.

Just where the sheds in this picture were situated I have been unable to fathom, though the church in the background is a good clue. The consensus of opinion is that they stood near the corner of Church Road and Whites Lane and, though hidden by new houses, some are still there. I am told that they were probably the net sheds of the Star Drift Fishing Company.

It may be that some of the sheds are still standing. Though most of them are gone, there are still beating sheds scattered about the village, but none is still in use for the old trade They have been converted to a number of different uses - offices, stores and even a car repair workshop. It is remarkable how these wooden buildings, some around a century old, have survived.

Photograph kindly loaned by Colin Eyre

The sight of them must bring back many memories for those who worked as beatsters. After the Ransacker had sorted out the damaged nets and handed them out to the various beatsters, the work would begin. Some required little work, a few with spronks, one mesh gone, or crow's feet, with three. Other nets were in tatters, bitten to pieces by dogfish - 'dog-eaten' as they were called. If they were too bad for mending they were thrown on one side for sale as garden lints.

Mending nets was, in those days, quite a cottage industry in the village. Wives with a family could not work full-time so they worked at home, a shed in the garden doing service as a beating shed. Often they had an oil cooker in the shed so that they could work and keep an eye on the dinner at the same time!

Before the last war, I was told, a home worker would be paid five shillings for each net, but after the war it went up to £1 - money hard-earned. Everyone seemed to grumble that they always got the worst of the nets!

The war meant the end of herring fishing off East Anglia, but the beatsters were not idle. They turned their hands and skills to camouflage nets. The Army had an insatiable demand for these nets which, festooned with shreds of material were thrown over tanks, guns, lorries and other equipment.

After the war the beatsters were back on the herring nets, but it was not to last for long. The great herring shoals which had been a basis for prosperity for centuries faded away and with them a whole tradition based upon them at ports and villages all along the coast.

The drifters have gone and the net drying grounds on Lowestoft Denes have been taken over by caravans, but at Kessingland the old beating sheds remain to bring back memories of the days when the herring was King.

HARVEST OF THE SEA

There will be no difficulty in recognising this old picture the interior of St. Edmund's Church. This was the occasion on January 11th 1953 when the first Harvest of the Sea service since the War was held in the church. The Rector at that time was the Rev John Fountain Page, pictured here against the background of flags, lifebelts and nets.

Kessingland Church has a long history of Harvest of the Sea services, being one of the first in the country to hold them. The Rev Tupper Carey, Rector of Lowestoft early this century, is credited with the idea of such celebrations. The workers on the land had long enjoyed their Harvest Festivals, why shouldn't the fishermen have theirs. So he organised the first Harvest of the Sea to take place early in the year after the ending of the herring voyage.

Tupper Carey was regarded as a fisherman's parson and despite the fact that pigs and parsons were regarded as taboo on fishing boats he often went to sea on Lowestoft trawlers and drifters. Just why pigs and parsons were regarded as an ill omen no-one seems to know, but they were certainly held in some dread.

I well remember when I first went to sea on a minesweeping trawler out of Lowestoft being very forcibly told by the old fishing skipper that I was not to speak of pigs. If I did have to refer to them, I was to call them 'curly tails'. As for parsons, I was to speak of 'the man in the black suit'. He was deadly serious about it! I never spoke of them again!

Some fishing skippers were in such dread of pigs that they would not allow pork or bacon on board their boats.

There was, however, an antidote to some landlubber like myself talking about pigs and parsons. The dread consequences could be fended off by murmuring 'cold iron' all the more potent if one could grip a bit of iron at the same time!

But all that was on board ship. Ashore the parson was treated with great friendliness and Harvest of the Sea services were packed.

But even so it was a wise parson who chose his Biblical texts with care. One mention of swine and he might find himself with an empty church!

COAL

Village life in the 17th and 18th centuries was pretty basic. There were none of the amenities we know today - electricity, gas, sewers and mains water. What was life like for the average villager in those days? How did they manage without those services which we take so much for granted? For the answer one does not have to go back down the centuries - merely to talk to people who lived in Kessingland before the war. They had none of these amenities, indeed, in that respect, domestic life had shown little advance since the 17th century! The only improvements were coal fires and oil cooking stoves and lamps.

Two hundred years ago coal was virtually unknown, at least among the poor, their main fuel was 'flaggs', of turf cut from the common lands which surrounded the village and which they burned rather like peat. The Overseer's accounts list many deliveries of flaggs, indeed, it was not uncommon for a widow to receive several thousands of them during the year. These are a few random entries over the period: Cutting 4000 flaggs for ye poor 13s 4d Carting & stacking them - and beer - 12s Set1800 flaggs for Goody Elmer 5s and carrying them 3s 6d Graving 2000 flaggs for ye poor 6s 8d. It is interesting to note that the digging of such turf is variously described as 'graving', 'cutting' or 'forking'. In each case a different implement was used.

Graving meant the use of a special spade known as a Becket. Cutting was done with a machette and in the other method a broad-bladed fork was used. In addition to flaggs. there were also deliveries of bundles of furze and broom, and small quantities of wood. These would have been used to get the turf blazing, and also in the large brick ovens which were used for baking. They were heated by lighting a fire inside and keeping it going until the bricks were glowing hot. The ashes were then scraped out, the inside was swabbed out with a wet mop. In went the dough and the oven was sealed. There was considerable heat left after the bread had been baked enabling other food which did not require such great heat to be cooked - perhaps a batch of the famous Suffolk rusks.

Few small cottages had these brick ovens, but there was one at the Town House which was available to the poor and this was probably used on a rota system. An interesting entry in 1735 reveals the first delivery of coal to one of the poor: "A Chaldron of coal for Widow Barber £1 4s". It was the first, and last, delivery of coal in the period covered by the accounts. A Chaldron was originally a measure of volume and when used for coal it meant a little over a ton.

Thus Widow Barber's coal worked out at about £1 a ton. Compare this with per ton of coal over the past century:

The experiment of providing coal for Widow Barber was not repeated and the villagers went on burning turf. As the Suffolk poet George Crabbe says in *The Village*:

"Lo where the heath, with withering brake grown o'er lands the tight turf which warms the neighbouring poor"

Year	£1
1900	£1.30
1910	£1.30
1920	£3.00
1930	£2.50
1940	£2.60
1950	£5.50
1960	£10
1970	£19
1980	£80
1984	£102
1994	£140

Turf burns quite well as I discovered in an experimental fire from some which I had stacked up in my garden it glowed and smouldered, but gave off enough heat to boil a small can of water. Mine was. of course, a very small fire. In practice, I imagine, turf fires were kept well piled up and were kept burning continuously. At an inn in the West Country I am told, there is a peat fire which has been burning for at least 200 years! The vast acres of common land which surrounded the villages, providing fuel and grazing for all the inhabitants, began to disappear in the 18th century when they were enclosed, mainly by the large landowners and we owe our familiar pattern of hedged fields to this change

Kessingland's common land was enclosed in 1786 when it was shared out between land and property owners with a value of over £5 a year. There were great outcries over the whole of the country about the poor being 'robbed' of their common rights:

"The fault is great in man or woman who steals a goose from off the Common but what can plead that man's excuse who steals the common off the goose?"

This was one of the bitter jibes of the period. Greatly concerned about the threat to the supply of fuel. Kessingland's Overseers prevailed upon the Enclosure Commissioners to safeguard at least some of the rights of the poor. As a result the Commissioners set aside 35 acres of land on Rothenhall Heath as a perpetual trust in the hands of the Lord of the Manor, the Vicar, Churchwardens and overseers, and their successors, in perpetuity, to provide firing for the poor. In addition, these Trustees were empowered to decide how this was done.

As coal began to be accepted as a more suitable fuel, it was found more convenient to have the land farmed along with the adjoining heath and to use the rent for providing coal. Eventually, with the ever-rising cost of coal, this was no longer economic, but still the benefits of that Trust of over 200 years ago continue to help the village. This legacy from those good -hearted Overseers continues with the Kessingland Help in Need Trust enabling it to carry on the good work which has gone on down the centuries. We owe a debt of gratitude to those unpaid Overseers who cared so much - and to those who have carried on their spirit.

Widow Barber's coal was probably landed from a wherry at Mutford Bridge and delivered by horse and cart - a mode of transport which changed little until the closing years of the last century. Billy Cooper with his cart pulled by two donkeys Obadiah and Malachi - was a local character. When one of his donkeys dropped dead when pulling a load up Pleasurewood Hill, he was flabbergasted.

"I've never known it to do that afore" he said.

OVER WHELMED!

It is, I see from my diary, just thirty years ago this month that the great local pastime of 'going down the fish market' came to an end. It was in January 1960 that Lowestoft harbour master Bob Owen fenced in the fish market and declared it a no-go area. There had, of course, been previous attempts to end the free for all on the quayside.

In 1912 there had been a campaign by the fishing firms for the market to be closed to the general public. They wanted to get rid of the 'juveniles and loafers' who swarmed on the quays, particularly during the herring season, helping themselves to fish which littered the landings. The Great Eastern Railway, however, refused to introduce a ban.

It was a freedom which lasted well after the end of the last war. All and sundry thronged the market as the herring baskets swung the catches ashore. Anything which fell from the baskets

Scots Fisher girls at work during the great East Anglian herring voyage

was regarded as fair game. People with vast bags scooped up the harvest of the sea and there were even those who ran a shuttle service with old prams between the quayside and local smokehouses.' It was a great herring bonanza and the whole town felt that it had a right to share in it.

Even when the herring season was over the fish market was still regarded as a free for all, but obviously it could not last for ever. Various attempts were made to restrict access. Holidaymakers were a particular problem during the summer but one official excuse for keeping them at bay badly misfired. Girls in bikinis, it was claimed, were a dangerous distraction for the filleters with their razor-sharp knives. A moment's distraction, it was said, could cause a nasty accident! It was the filleters themselves who put an end to that particular ploy. It was a risk, they announced, which they were more than willing to take! But finally, in January 1960, it all came to an end. The market was closed to the general public and it became a more orderly, if less interesting place.

What else does my diary reveal from Januaries of the past?

Rationing is one potent memory. It was on January 8th, 1940, that we all had to start registering with our grocers and butchers for supplies of rationed foodstuffs 12 ounces of sugar, 4 ounces of bacon, and around 2 pounds of meat a week. The ration went up and down, usually down, as the war went on until there was very little which one could buy without a ration book or coupons. Rationing was to last until the 1950s when we could forget all about checking on our 'total calorie intake' that is until the great slimming vogue arrived on the scene

WHETHER THE WEATHER ...

Talk about the 'Greenhouse Effect' though some of us doubt the theory has lulled most of us into expecting mild winters, particularly after we had escaped from January.

The snow and the severe frosts, therefore, took us all rather by surprise. Perhaps that will teach us not to be so complacent in the future, and to remember the old East Anglian adage 'As the days lengthen so the cold strengthen!"

Most of the blizzards and mini 'ice ages' of the past seem to have surprised us almost as much as the recent snow confounded British Rail! That memorable winter of 1947. for instance, did not start until January 23rd just when most of us were declaring that it was all down hill to Spring. And it went on and on. Even the sea froze as the freeze and blizzards continued. There was plenty of fun about as the Broads froze and on one Sunday morning there were over 3000 skaters at Oulton Broad. The ice here was so thick that people took to driving onto the frozen Broad. It was a remarkable sight, but drivers became more cautious when one man returned to his car to find that he had parked on a weak spot and his vehicle had disappeared.... The general thaw did not set in till March 15th.

Just a century ago East Anglia was suffering from another of the ice ages. Then the great freeze began in early December 1890 and lasted till the end of January '91. In mid-January it was reported that there were 5000 skaters out on Oulton Broad, many drawn, no doubt, by the spectacle of a sheep being roasted out on the ice. It seemed to have been a festive occasion with sleigh rides round the Broad at thru'pence a time, all the money going to Lowestoft Hospital.

But, as on all such occasions there was misery and hardship for many. Soup kitchens were set up in many towns and villages to feed the hungry and it was reported that in Lowestoft alone they were serving as many as 600 people a day.

The Book of Dates which I have compiled shows Januarys of the past littered with great storms, blizzards. floods and severe frosts.

On January 7th, 1877, for instance, nine Lowestoft smacks sank with all hands. They were *Dove. Flying Foam, Enterprise. William and Sarah, Kingfisher, William and Ann, Emily. Langford and Protector.* A few days later five more were lost *John and Emma, Prince of Wales. Semper Paratus. Star of Peace and Fidget.* Perhaps we should not grumble too much when we are surprised by a sudden cold snap in winter!

I don't wish to be gloomy, but perhaps I should point out, however, that we are not out of the wood yet. On May 3rd 1968, Suffolk was hit by a blizzard which went on for the best part of the afternoon'

On the subject of unusual weather, let me end with the story of an extraordinary happening at Easter 1929. Alfred Glenn described it in his book *'Weather Patterns of East Anglia'* "At sunset on Good Friday a shining cross appeared in the sky directly above the dying sun. It was hailed as a miracle by the many awe-inspired witnesses who were promptly put in their place by know-alls explaining that it was nothing more than a sun pillar caused by light reflected off ice crystals in the upper atmosphere, intersected by a short band of high cirrus cloud illuminated by the sun!

"But if a 'miracle¹ can be factually explained does that make it any less wonderful?"

EATING AND DRINKING

The fishermen of Suffolk have always enjoyed a reputation for being hearty trenchermen, and in the days when herring were still abundant the crews of drifters managed to eat their way through quite an appreciable proportion of the catch. The cook of the Lowestoft drifter *Girl Margaret,* for example decided one morning to count the number of herring he fried for the crew. Ten men sat down to breakfast that day and when they finally pushed aside their plates they had managed to get through 120 fish between them.

Those who took part in that particular meal did not content themselves with eating only the succulent back portion of the fish. They ate the lot, apart from the bones, and managed to tuck away a fair ration of bread apiece besides. What was no doubt regarded by the men as a tasty little snack with which to start the day was washed down with mugs of hot steaming tea always one of the major requirements on the fishing grounds.

Such hearty eaters would have had little difficulty in beating the Fraserburgh man who claimed a world record not so many years ago after eating a mere dozen kippers in fifteen minutes.

The cook of one Lowestoft smack could recall frying a bucketful of fish for a single meal. Small plaice, gurnards and weevers found their way into the pan together with soles and plaice, and each man in the crew took between a dozen and eighteen fish as a first helping. It was, according to the cook in question, an awe-inspiring sight to see the men tucking into these great mounds of fish, with the meal liberally sprinkled with vinegar and mustard sauce.

No Suffolk fish eating championship was ever organised officially, but outstanding feats were now and again recorded and passed into local legend. Among the most remarkable of these achievements were those attributed to the Lowestoft fisherman Amos Beamish the "giant of Barnby" who was reckoned to regularly eat thirty herring at a sitting. Perhaps it was his healthy liking for a fish diet which helped Amos to achieve and maintain his size and strength. Even among the fishing fraternity, where there is no shortage of big, strong men, Amos achieved an enviable reputation. When he served on drifters it was said of him that on one vessel the hatchway had to be specially enlarged so that he could ease his great bulk down to the cabin. But owners were always glad to have him on board as a member of the crew, for he was able to do the work of two normal men.

On one occasion, for a bet, Amos ate a really fantastic meal, when he got through one hundred spring herring. But he met his match that day, for sitting at the table with him was one "Scarlet" Bryant who somehow managed to eat one hundred and one fish.

There was a time when many Lowestoft drifters went to Newlyn to take part in the mackerel fishery, and it was during one of these westward voyages that the Barnby giant added further laurels to his reputation as a man of outstanding strength. That was when he took on the local champion and each man attempted to lift a rock weighing over 60 stone. Beamish took a firm grip on the great boulder and lifted it with hardly a grunt. His opponent could not budge it when his turn came.

His most remarkable feat of strength was at the time of the Barnby train disaster at Christmas, 1891. Amos was one of the first people on the scene of the crash, which happened a short distance from his home, and he worked tirelessly in helping to free people trapped in the wreckage. One account of the rescue work said: "Foremost was Mr. Amos Beamish, a man of almost gigantic strength, which he turned to such good account as to make one almost believe it was specially increased for the occasion". Legend has it that alone he lifted the end of one coach to free the people trapped beneath.

Like many of his fellow fishermen, Amos Beamish was particularly fond during his time at sea of a meal consisting of fish taken straight from the net, cleaned and popped into the pan. The cooking technique he knew was rough and ready but the outcome was a dish as tasty and succulent as could be found in the finest kitchens ashore.

On board a typical drifter of his time the herring destined for the table would be swiftly gutted,

then "topped and tailed" and slashed along each side with a jack-knife before being consigned to the frying pan. Served up piping hot the fish would be eaten by the crew with their fingers. Cutlery tended to be in short supply on the old time fishing vessels and, in any event, eating in this way left a hand clear to stop the plate sliding around too much.

Fish can be prepared for the table in an immense variety of ways, however, and in any seafaring community people will be found who will swear that one particular method of preparation is superior to any other. No fish has been given more attention in this respect than the herring and even today, when the great shoals of the past are a fading memory, Suffolk people still eagerly await such tasty delicacies as the first "North Shields kippers" of the summer months, or the hard to come by "red" herrings.

In Victorian times kippers were a regular feature of the breakfast menu, though their popularity began to suffer during the first world war after the introduction of "painted ladies" which owed their colouring to dye rather than to smoke. One of many bids to increase the popularity of kippers came during the 1930's, when people were urged to eat a kipper a day for the sake of their health. There were even plans to introduce herring bars to rival the milk bars which were then enjoying considerable business. But the idea never really caught on.

There is, nevertheless, still a considerable demand even today for kippers prepared in the traditional way by smoking, preferably over a fire of oak chips. Over 3,000 people wrote to a Lowestoft man who offered a few years ago to tell them where they could obtain the old fashioned kind of kipper.

The eating of red herrings tends to be something more of an acquired taste, as they retain their saltiness even after prolonged soaking. But raw red herring cut into thin slices can be served up on toast as a more than acceptable substitute for smoked salmon.

Another salty offering which at one time formed an important part of the diet for poorer families was the pickle-cured herring. One recommended method of dealing with these fish was to soak them for a minimum of two days, changing the water several times and then to boil them (changing the water twice) and finally serve the fish with a mustard sauce. Even this treatment, however, was reckoned to leave the fish with a distinctly salty flavour.

A more acceptable way of dealing with pickled herring was to soak them for four days, changing the water daily. On the fourth day the herrings were split, the bone removed and the fish fried like a bloater until crisp. Variations on these methods of cooking have been tried out for generations, and as long ago as the mid-16th century one writer recorded of herrings that "some use them (when the backbone is withdrawn) with onions, apples, vinegar and oil, also roasted, or watered, and broiled".

Writing just over a century ago the historian John Greaves Nail said: "Of all fish that swim in the sea, none has been more bountifully and abundantly supplied by a wise providence for the sustenance of man than the herring; and, considering its cheapness, its excellent flavour and wholesomeness, no article of diet has undergone so absurd a prescription from the tables of the wealthy and great".

The "wealthy and great" who in Nail's day scorned the herring as a dish certainly did not follow the example of their predecessors, for many Royal households feasted upon herring pies during the centuries when red herrings from East Anglia were a staple item of diet. Over 450 years ago Norwich was bound to supply 24 herring pies each year to the sovereign's household by way of rent though the citizens fell somewhat from grace in the year 1629 when the pies were found not to measure up to the required standard.

Curiously, while sophisticated diners turned away from the herring in this country during the 1800's perhaps because other varieties of fish were more readily available than in former times things were very different on the other side of the English Channel. French chefs excelled themselves in producing a wide range of appetising recipes in which the herring was duly accorded a place of honour.

It was one of these French chefs who devised a breakfast worthy of satisfying the heartiest of appetites when he advised cooks to first select "eight fine red herrings". The heads and tails of the fish had to be removed, together with the skin and backbone. Next, the herring were filleted and placed in a sheet of well buttered paper, with the fillets separated by a morsel of fresh butter, mixed with sweet herbs, some mushrooms, parsley, shallots, pepper and olive oil. After being sprinkled with bread crumbs the fish was cooked slowly and served very hot with the addition of lemon juice.

"We request our honourable readers", said the "Almanach des Gourmands", "to make trial of this recipe in one of those moments of leisure, when the imagination loves to create new enjoyments for the stomach, and we will venture to believe that they will thank us for calling their attention to it".

When it comes to present day methods of dealing with fresh herring "preferably acquired 'stiff alive' " a great many East Anglian cooks hold that it is cheating somewhat to place the fish under the grill. A favourite Lowestoft dish is to clean the herring and then "snotch" the sides with three or four deep cuts to ensure that the fish is thoroughly cooked. The herring are then rolled in flour and gently fried though as a variation some prefer to dispense with the flour and place the fish directly into piping hot fat in the pan. The secret of even cooking is to put the herrings in the pan with their bellies facing the cook. The fish will then roll over far more easily when the time comes to turn them.

So appetising is the long list of tasty fish meals available today that it is hard to imagine the kind of fare served up in the distant past, when the food provided for fishermen on their way to the grounds would consist very largely of salted or dried cod. These additions to the menu became known as "sea beef and their palatability can be judged from the fact that it was standard procedure to soften a chunk of this cod by stretching it across an anchor and then thumping it with a heavy metal spike.

Real salt beef was also taken aboard the old time vessels in large quantities, though menus had improved somewhat by the time the hey-day of the East Anglian ports had arrived. A meal such as was served then would be quite acceptable to people today and would, perhaps, include a hefty joint of mutton or beef, served up with a plentiful supply of gravy, potatoes and the ever-present dumplings. It was honest, simple fare, dished up in quantities sufficient to satisfy the appetites of men who might have been hauling nets without a break for a matter of 14 hours or more.

Not all owners, of course, were over mindful of the need for good food aboard their vessels, and at least one Lowestoft man, looking back to the days when he became the 13-year-old cook on a local smack in the 1880's, recalled that the only meat taken on board was salt beef. Sea biscuits there were in plenty, though these would on occasion be riddled with weevils which were dealt with by dropping the biscuit into a hot mug of tea and then flicking out the weevils as they floated to the surface with the tip of a finger.

At one time, provisions for fishing vessels working from ports such as Lowestoft would also include large quantities of beer doubtless to help wash away some of the taste of a salt dominated diet. But as the years went by another drink emerged which has held its place among favourite beverages at sea. It is the humble cup of tea, invariably served up "hot, strong and sweet", and constantly available from any well-ordered galley.

The Herring Season, Lowestoft

In the small but admirable maritime museum which is to be found in Sparrow's Nest gardens at Lowestoft there is an exhibit which demonstrates this partiality among fishermen for tea. It is a huge kettle and its capacity is two gallons. When it was in use a kettle like this would be kept constantly on the boil, with a generous measure of tea being tipped in now and again according to requirements. Old leaves remained in the kettle until such time as some had to be removed to make way for sufficient water. And when the brew was poured condensed milk was regarded as far and away the favourite sweetener.

Good food and plenty of it. That has been the maxim which has kept generations of Suffolk fishermen contented at meal-times and a good cook has always been held in high esteem. Stores taken aboard one of the sailing smacks in the days of fleeting, when the vessel would be at sea for as long as eight weeks at a time, included such commodities as plenty of currants and raisins, together with hefty consignments of beef, flour and cheese. Perhaps to help mask the taste of the culinary efforts of inexpert young cooks supplies then also included a healthy ration of mustard, pepper and salt, and bottles of relish.

And what about the fishermen of today? On board the latest trawlers sailing from Lowestoft meal times are as flexible as ever but crew members enjoy menus which would have been beyond the wildest dreams of their predecessors. Modern technology has brought with it the introduction of deep freeze equipment, and this in turn means that on an up-to-date trawler food such as fresh meat and bread can be provided throughout the voyage.

Cereal, eggs and bacon for breakfast is commonplace nowadays. For a main meal soup will be followed by meat beef, pork or lamb and chicken at least once a week. A full range of vegetables, fresh or canned, also comes from the galley and for a sweet course the wide choice may even include a generous serving of ice-cream. High tea, with salads in season and plenty of cheese and biscuits, helps contribute further to the well-being of the men who work the North Sea grounds on Lowestoft trawlers. To wash down their meals they can have a choice of

liberal supplies of tea, coffee or cocoa, and some trawlers are equipped with refrigerated machines serving cool drinks.

However, despite all the improvements in available foods and cooking methods one dish has never been displaced as a favourite among the fishermen. It consists simply of a plate heaped high with fried fish served hot from the galley for breakfast.

PEPY'S LIGHT

It would be a waste of time we have the assurance of Trinity House on this point to try to establish which is the oldest lighthouse in the British Isles, but there is little doubt that Lowestoft would be among the main contenders. Few towns in the country can boast of a longer connection with the history and growth of coastal lights than this most easterly point in the country.

The present lighthouse is now getting on for a century old, but the story of Lowestoft's lights goes back over three and a half centuries back to the days of coal fires and candles which guided seamen through the narrow and constantly shifting Stanford Channel.

Having claimed, in another chapter of this book, that Lowestoft is "the cradle of the lifeboat service", it would, perhaps, be a little greedy to take the credit for the first lighthouse too! But one thing is certain, the earliest record of the building of a lighthouse in this country was that at Lowestoft in 1609.

It is known that there were lights of some kind at Caister, north of Great Yarmouth, and that these were taken over by Trinity House in 1600, but it is not clear whether they were lighthouses. Apparently Trinity House has some difficulty in maintaining these lights. The official keeper farmed out the job of lighting the candles to an old woman who lived some distance away. Consequently, the worse the weather the less likely it was that she would be able to make the journey to get the candles going.

Lowestoft appears to be the first light built by Trinity House. Winterton and Dungeness lights were established in 1615 and the Forelands and Orfordness in 1634. Of course, there were warning lights long before this bonfires, braziers and beacons on the headlands to help the mariners. The remains of one such beacon are still to be seen just inside the entrance of Belle Vue Park at Lowestoft, a short distance from the present lighthouse. Until Belle Vue Park was laid out towards the end of the last century, this was waste land looking out over the sea, an ideal place for a beacon.

No one has been able to put a date on this pile of old flints. but it is thought that they are at least four centuries old. There is a local legend that these old stones are a potent rain-maker. All one has to do is to pour a bucket of water over them at midnight to be sure of a deluge of rain within the next 24 hours! Legend also has it that these stones are so thirsty for water that at certain times of the year, at dead of night, naturally, they go down to the beach for a bathe!

The unreliable beacon was replaced by a lighthouse which was built in 1609 and by the end of that century there were only 15 in England, six in Ireland and one in Scotland.

Samuel Pepys, the famous diarist, was responsible for the building of the next lighthouse at Lowestoft. As Master of Trinity House he ordered, in 1676, the building of a brick and stone lighthouse and this is commemorated by a plaque which was set up at that time and which is

still to be seen inside the present building. The plaque reads: "Erected by the Brotherhood of the Trinity House of Deptford Strond in the Mastership of Samuel Pepys Esq., Secretary of ye Admiralty of England. A.D. 1676." Beneath are the Arms of Trinity House and a scroll bearing their motto *"Trinitas in Unitale"*. This lighthouse was 40 feet high and 20 feet in diameter. Gillingwater. the Lowestoft historian, writing in 1790. tells us that the top part, about 30 feet from the ground, had been sashed on the seaward side to give protection to the hearth where a coal fire was kept burning continuously every night.

Gillingwater also tells us that in 1777. when the upper part of the structure became so much decayed that it was necessary to have it repaired, the Brethren of Trinity House resolved to take the top wholly off and erect in its place one of the newly-invented reflecting cylinders. This was done and the old coal fire was replaced by oil burners. Having found that the new system was a great success. Trinity House promptly dismantled the whole thing and shipped it out to the Scilly Isles and Lowestoft went back to the old coal fire. But the town got the new system a year later.

As well as being more reliable and giving a better light, the oil burning lights were also much cheaper than coal. The vast coal fires consumed huge quantities of fuel and the coal bill for the year amounted to £500 a colossal sum for those days. Further repairs and improvements were carried out in 1825 and 1840, but by about 1870 it was obvious that the old lighthouse, then nearly 200 years old, was doomed.

The Pepy's lighthouse was replaced by a new one which was opened on February 16, 1874, having been built during the previous year. It had a dioptric lantern lit by oil and oil continued to be the fuel till the coming of electricity in 1938.

Today the light is lit by electricity from the public supply and there are stand-by batteries in case this fails. In the event of any failure the system is automatically switched to the batteries and a warning sounds to alert the keeper. So important is the maintenance of the light that there is a third stand-by, a petrol driven generator and in the event of all three failing at the same time there is a reserve supply of oil lamps. Presumably if the worst comes to the worst and even the oil lamps fail to function the keeper starts burning his shirt or turns the clock back two centuries and lights a coal fire!

Modern automatic systems and alarms means that it is no longer necessary for there to be more than one keeper at Lowestoft lighthouse. The clockwork which rotates the lantern in its bath of mercury will operate for 12 hours once it has been wound, and once set in motion the light is switched on and off by a time switch.

The days when there was a head keeper and two assistants have long since passed and Lowestoft lighthouse is now a man and wife station as it is called in the service. It is one of the few lighthouses where a man can have his wife and family with him and, standing in the main street, with buses stopping at the door, it is usually a welcome relief from the more isolated lights though some keepers do complain about the noise of the traffic!

The nature of the light has not always remained as it is now. It is now a revolving light, there being one white flash of 0.3 of a second every 15 seconds. Before the installation of electricity it was a much longer flash of two seconds repeated at 30 second intervals.

Another adaptation was required at the lighthouse in 1968 when Lowestoft Corporation built a new tower block of flats a short distance away. Tenants whose windows looked out on the lighthouse complained about the flash which lit up their bedrooms every 15 seconds. An understanding Trinity House promptly added extra screening to the light.

Although it has been part of their life for well over 300 years, Lowestoft people never refer to the lighthouse. It is always "The Highlight", a reminder of the days when the town had two lighthouses the one on the cliff which exists today and the other, "The Lowlight" on the beach. Between them the two lights guided ships through the Stanford Channel, the lowlight being moved from time to time to keep in line with the ever-wandering channel.

The first lowlight was lit by candles and when Baskerville visited the town in 1681, he mentioned "two watch or light houses, one for candle and the other a great fire of coal". The candle-lit beacon stood at the bottom of Swan's Score, now known as Mariners' Score. Gillingwater records that in 1735 a movable timber-framed lighthouse was erected on the beach "whose construction admitted of its being moved according to the movement of the channel, which was at that time generally northerly". He goes on to say that in 1779 the timber was found to be so decayed that the building was taken down and replaced by another of the same type. The lowlight had by then moved to the beach near Spurgeon's Score, and it made many more moves during the next 100 years as it tried to keep pace with the restless Stanford Channel.

In 1867 the old wooden structure was replaced by one of tubular steel which was still capable of being moved about the beach and it was not until 1922, when better buoyage of the channel had made it unnecessary, that the lowlight was dispensed with.

Another wandering lighthouse was the one which now stands, disused, in the grounds of Pontin's holiday camp to the south of Pakefield. This was originally built at Corton in 1870, later moved to Kessingland and then pulled down and transported to Pakefield. When it was again decided to move it in 1910 it was hauled lock stock and barrel to its present site no mean feat as it weighed in the region of 70 tons!

It was some considerable time after lighthouses had become a recognised aid to navigation that thought was given to lightships at sea. Until well into the 18th century, with the exception of a small number of buoys and a few beacons on sandbanks, there was nothing to help the mariner once he was out of sight of land. Negotiating the intricate and treacherous channels off the East Coast was a tricky business without a light to help.

Then, in 1732, a floating light was placed in the Nore. It was the idea of a King's Lynn man, Robert Hamblin, and at first the scheme did not meet with a great deal of success. The vessel, which showed candles in a lantern, was continually dragging anchor and being carried away. But the idea caught on and gradually the curiously shaped lightships became part of the mariner's way of life.

Lowestoft's own particular lightship for getting on for a century was the Corton, but she was replaced in 1968 by a "monster" buoy. It is not known quite how long the Corton had been on station before she was replaced by an unmanned buoy, but she was certainly not there in 1866. In that year Nail published his guide to Yarmouth and Lowestoft, an exhaustive tome which runs to over 700 pages and which covers a wide range of topics, including lightships off the coast.

Corton lightship is not listed, but Nail does record two which have since been taken out of service. They were the St. Nicholas Gall lightship which marked the fairway between the Scroby and Corton sands, and the Stanford lightship, which was stationed near the north end of the Newcombe sands and which guided vessels through the Stanford channel to Lowestoft harbour. The St. Nicholas went on station in 1837 and the Stanford in 1815.

The Corton station is roughly midway between these two and it appears that some time after 1866 Trinity House decided that one lightship could do the job of two and the Corton station was established.

Nail gives some interesting details about service on the lightships. The lights in those days were oil-burners, the lanterns costing in the region of £300. The Calrophic lantern on the Stanford had eight burners and in 1858 it consumed 604 gallons of oil and 145 dozen wicks. The crew must have spent most of their time changing the wicks.

In those days, warning in fog was given by a huge bell weighing nearly three cwt. and worked by automatic machinery. The whole installation cost £240 and it was claimed that it could be heard for four miles. Life on board must have been particularly trying during foggy weather.

As an alternative to the bells, Trinity House once tried out the idea of Chinese gongs which were said to be particularly penetrating. Gongs were supplied to a number of lightships and the crews were instructed to beat them continuously during thick weather. But they proved a failure.

Time usually hung rather heavily for the men of the lightships before the days of television and radio and most of them occupied themselves with a hobby. Nail records that it was a saving of those days: "Wait for the relief of a lightship and you can get anything from a chest of drawers to a penny whistle". The light-men of those days received £2 15s. a month, rising to £5 if they achieved the status of skipper. Out of this they had to find their own provisions and take their turn at the cooking. Not surprisingly, they took advantage of their position to do a bit of fishing to supplement their diet, but they also had an unusual supply of food the birds which dashed themselves against the lantern. The light, with its eight oil burners, was a magnet to birds of all sorts chiefly starlings, thrushes, blackbirds and woodcocks. It was recorded, says Nail, that on one single night 1.000 birds killed themselves by crashing into the lights on the Newarp lightship which had three lanterns.

"At six o'clock in the morning" writes Nail, "the crew began to make an enormous sea-pie into which they put 600 birds, and what with the plucking them, and cooking the pie it was six in the evening before dinner was announced.

Birds, of course. still come to grief against the lanterns of the lightships and all bird-lovers will rejoice as the lightships are replaced by the new "monster" buoys which are less likely to lure them to their doom.

PLEASE DON'T MENTION PIGS - OR PARSONS

Pictures show the Rev. Tupper-Carey with fishermen

Strange beliefs and superstitions abound in seafaring communities in many parts of the world, and among the East Anglian fishermen there are still many who firmly adhere to customs and sayings, the origins of which have long since been forgotten.

How. for instance, did the custom begin of throwing overboard a handful of small coins at the start of the voyage to "buy a good catch". There are fishermen sailing from the port of Lowestoft today who follow this custom, just as did previous generations of local fishermen.

Why do they do it? They cannot give any rational explanation it is simply something that has always been done, and to ignore it would be to run the risk of having to return to port with a poor catch to show for their pains.

This particular belief seems to have been much more deeply rooted a hundred years ago. when some Lowestoft fishermen held that bad luck would follow if they were to take copper coins to sea at all. As soon as they were discovered the pennies and halfpennies would be hastily thrown over the side no small sacrifice in the days when the earnings of fishermen were pitifully low.

One possible explanation of this aversion to having small change on board is to be found in the very old belief that an effigy of a horse worked in copper would bring bad luck. The story has come down of a failure in the Norwegian herring voyage one year long ago, when the disaster was attributed to the poisoning of the sea after a copper horse was thrown into the water. As time went on this tale could well have given rise to a widely held superstitious awe of copper effigies of any kind and, in turn, to coins made of copper. It may be fanciful but how else can one explain what by now must be a sizeable fortune in small coins literally thrown away to be scattered on the bed of the North Sea.

Coins, however, were not the only articles to go over the side in attempts to bring good luck or avert bad. Some skippers at one time thought it was unlucky to have a pocket watch on board, and there is at least one recorded instance of a skipper who threw his own watch into the sea after a poor catch.

If any headgear accidentally blew over the side, it was believed among many fisherman that this was not only an instance of bad luck for the unfortunate loser but that it also heralded a longer fishing trip than usual.

Another way of supposedly bringing good luck was well-known to some of the Scottish fishermen who formerly voyaged to East Anglia in their hundreds for the autumn fishing. In at least one of their home ports it was the curious custom before the start of the voyage to dress a cooper in a flannel shirt and to stick burrs all over the garment before pulling the man through the streets seated in a wheelbarrow. Presumably the idea was to make good fortune stick to the cooper, whose work depended on the success of the fishermen.

Among the same communities it was thought to be most unlucky to meet anyone with the surname White when going to join a ship and on the other side of the North Sea there was the well-founded belief that it was unlucky to envy good fortune experienced by others.

All manner of everyday objects have been the subject of superstitious beliefs, from the humble loaf of bread to a stone with a hole in it. The stones were avoided because they were supposed to signify that fish would escape through the mesh of the net, though this could be counter-balanced by the fisherman with the forethought to keep a little salt in his possession. Apart from stones pierced with holes white stones were also avoided because of their associations with bad luck, and old smack fishermen would carefully go through bags of ballast now and again to remove any such stones. As for the bread, it was laid down very firmly in fishing lore that one of the unluckiest things a man could do was to cut a slice from the loaf and then turn it bottom up on the plate. That, it was said, was tantamount to inviting the ship to turn over during the voyage.

Turning the ship over could also come about if anyone on board slept on his stomach, said some, though it is to be doubted if any fisherman coming off watch would chance the wrath of a shipmate by waking him up to tell him of the offence. It would be a different matter on deck, of course, if a member of the crew were so incautious as to upturn a hatch cover a sure method of inviting disaster.

Two subjects which are definitely taboo on many fishing vessels even today are "pigs and parsons". The poor pig has long been held in superstitious dread among seafarers and the general prohibition on any mention of the animal led to its being referred to, if occasion arose, as merely "a curly tail".

There is a well authenticated story of a clergyman who visited a small fishing village and refused to believe the horror with which pigs were regarded. He learned a salutary lesson when he was invited to conduct a service in the local church and took as his text a biblical story in which there were several references to a herd of swine. The very first mention of the dreaded word caused a shudder of horror to pass through the congregation, and when it was repeated the worshippers turned to the only remedy they knew and began muttering the words "cold iron", which were reckoned to counter the awful effects of mention of pigs. Eventually, when the clergyman mentioned swine yet again the whole congregation is said to have fled from the church.

Such extreme fear of pigs is fortunately rare, but there are many who still believe that it is foolish to take chances and until a few years ago there was at least one Lowestoft fishing skipper who would never allow a joint of pork, or even a few rashers of bacon, on board his ship. And a member of the crew who dared to mention pigs in the skipper's hearing soon found himself seeking a berth elsewhere.

There were very strongly held superstitions, too, about the dangers of mentioning clergymen on board ship, and many old time skippers would have been moved almost to physical violence at the thought of actually having a clergyman set foot on his deck. The prohibition on clergymen took no account of position, and when the Bishop of Aberdeen and Orkney used to pay his annual visit to Lowestoft to meet the Scottish fishermen in port he was well aware of the tradition. It was his custom until a few years ago to take a gentle stroll around the quays, pausing now and then to chat for a few moments with the fishermen on board the drifters moored alongside. But he always made a point of never attempting to go on board any drifter.

A notable exception to this generally observed rule was provided by the Rev. Tupper-Carey, one time Rector of St. Margaret's Church, Lowestoft. He had a deep affection for the local fishermen, and won their confidence to such an extent that he was not only welcome to go on board the fishing boats and chat with the crews but was very often presented with gifts of fish. He was often to be seen cycling homewards to the Rectory with a string of fresh herring slung from his handlebars.

One of the most deeply rooted of the fishing superstitions of the past was that which said that an infallible charm against drowning was the ownership of a human caul (the hood of skin which is sometimes found enveloping a newly-born child). This somewhat bizarre object was dried and suspended in a little bag around the neck, and until quite recent times fishermen were prepared to pay very high prices indeed to buy such an object.

The "Morning Post" of August 21, 1779, carried a typical advertisement relating to this demand. It read: "To gentlemen of the Navy, and others going long voyages to sea. To be disposed of, a child's caul. Enquire at the Bartlett Buildings Coffee House in Holburn. N.B., to avoid unnecessary trouble, the price is twenty guineas".

Similar advertisements must have been familiar to Charles Dickens, for in "David Copperfield" he mentioned that his hero was born with a caul, "which was advertised for sale, in the newspapers, at the low price of fifteen guineas".

The belief in the efficacy of caul must by then have been on the wane, however, for the only offer was from an attorney who offered "two pounds in cash and the balance in sherry, but declined to be guaranteed from drowning on any higher bargain". At Lowestoft there was a sad echo of this old belief when Edward Archer, skipper of the smack *True Love,* was washed overboard and drowned in 1896, despite the fact that he was wearing a child's caul.

A curious example of a superstition which was not heeded when circumstances changed was the prohibition on board fishing vessels of any mention of rabbits. This did not prevent rabbits being taken on board on occasion   custom merely said that they should not be spoken of. When local fishermen were called up to join the Royal Navy during the second world war, they entered a society which had a vocabulary of its own. One of the words in that vocabulary was "rabbits"   slang for presents. And the inborn traditions of their own upbringing did not prevent the Lowestoft men from cheerfully asking their fellow ratings how many "rabbits" they were taking home to their families.

The old beliefs applied on shore as well as at sea, and woe betide the children of a superstitious fisherman who were caught whistling in the house, and by so doing were inviting a gale of wind to come along.

Even at the breakfast table superstition had a part to play, and at one time no housewife with a husband at sea would dream of throwing away an eggshell without first smashing it into tiny pieces. Half an eggshell, they believed, was enough to provide a craft suitable for a witch to sail on out to sea and bring disaster to the fleet.

Both on shore and at sea great significance is attached to the number 13, and for the fisherman the ill-fortune associated with this number has always been stronger if the date happens to be Friday the 13th. For one Lowestoft fisherman there was good cause to remember that date. On the first occasion he was on board a ship which sailed on Friday the 13th he was involved in an accident in which he fractured his skull. On the second occasion there was a fire on board. On the third occasion, when he was a member of the crew of the trawler *Granby Queen,* he arranged to meet the vessel at Yarmouth the following day. His subterfuge failed to work, and before the trip was over the trawler was involved in a dangerous, though successful, rescue at sea.

It might be thought that there would be some resistance among local owners to being assigned the registration number LT 13 for their craft, but this does not appear to be the case, and several vessels carrying this number appear in the old port records. The first seems to have been a sailing craft named *Isabella and Eliza,* which was listed between 1878 and 1884, but little is known about her or what was her eventual fate. Next to come along was the smack *Jane and Elizabeth,* built in 1885 for T. W. Reeve of Lowestoft and a winner of the local smack race in 1890. After a career of a quarter of a century this smack was eventually lost by fire in 1910 about 50 miles off her home port.

Seven years later the registration number LT 13 was once more taken up, this time by the longshore boat *General Wolfe.* For many years this boat had a successful career giving trips to holidaymakers and being used for longshoring. Still in existence, the *General Wolfe* is now honourably retired and is kept under a tarpaulin cover in a garden at Corton.

Yet another widespread belief among fishermen is that the wearing of a single gold ear-ring improves their eyesight. Lowestoft fishermen have long adopted the habit of wearing a simple gold ring in the lobe of one ear, and even though the custom is not as popular as it once was there are sufficient youngsters wearing them to ensure that this adornment will be seen around the harbour for many years to come.

In 1965, it is interesting to note, a 15-year-old Cumberland schoolboy was sent home from school because he was wearing a gold ring in one ear and his head master thought that it was "effeminate". The schoolboy in question was over 6 ft. tall and weighed some 16 stone and by now he is doubtless working alongside his fisherman father. It was an unfortunate choice to use the word effeminate in his case, and there is certainly nothing effeminate about the husky Lowestoft fishermen who also wear ear rings. The late Albert Spurgeon, a famous Lowestoft lifeboat coxswain wore a gold ear ring. And nobody would ever have dreamt of accusing that stalwart fisherman of being a "cissy".

Does wearing an ear ring really lead to improved vision? There may be no medical justification for the ancient belief but certainly many Lowestoft fishermen do have remarkable eyesight, and can pick out and name a vessel on the horizon when to the landlubber it may be little more than an indistinct blur.

THE ROARING BOYS AT BAY

The Story of Suffolk men against the sea contains many examples of selfless courage, skill and devotion to duty. It is a story which spans many centuries and one which will continue for as long as men seek their living from the sea. Some parts of the story are well-documented and the men and ships concerned have won a lasting place in the history of the ports from which they sailed. But for other parts there is no written record. No record, that is, except for the knowledge that some vessels have been lost without trace. And the secret of their fate is held fast by the brooding North Sea. The sea, however, can be challenged like any other powerful adversary, and there have always been men who have been ready to take up this challenge.

Such was the case one September night in the year 1918, when a group of veteran Lowestoft seamen snatched nine survivors from a stricken ship in the teeth of a savage north-easterly gale. That gale was at its height when the sloop *Pomona* was driven towards the shore five miles south of Southwold. The alarm was raised when flares fired from the stranded vessel were sighted - but for a time it seemed that nothing could be done to save the crew.

Conditions were too bad for the Aldeburgh lifeboat to put to sea. At Southwold the lifeboat *Albert Carry* had been condemned and a smaller boat at the station was clearly unequal to the demands of a rescue bid. An emergency call was flashed to Kessingland, but here too the lifeboat was unable to launch because not enough men were available.

Two hours after the signals of distress were sighted a call for assistance was put through to Lowestoft, where a ready response came from the men of the old Beach Village. Coxswain John Swan ran from house to house to help speed the assembly of a crew for the *Kentwell* lifeboat, and soon 18 brave men had mustered in readiness for a rescue attempt. The men who gathered that night were indeed veterans. No other men were available, for their sons had long left the town to join one or other of the Services but this was to be a night when experience would prove an asset as valuable as the presence of younger and stronger men.

When the lifeboat left Lowestoft harbour under sail just after 5 a.m. the crew included two men over 70 years of age. Twelve were over 60 and the remaining four were all over 50. Despite the heavy seas, the *Kentwell* reached the scene of the wreck two hours after setting out from Lowestoft. By this time the *Pomona* was hard aground some 300 yards from the shoreline. Waves were breaking constantly over the doomed vessel. Four seamen crouched on top of the wheelhouse and five more were clinging to the fore-rigging.

Coxswain Swan recorded in his personal log later: "We sailed in to her, but did not get fast the first time, so we tried again but did not succeed, so we tried again. Got fast this time to the fore-rigging with the grapnels and the men dropped into the boat as they got a chance".

The survivors who had clung to the wave- lashed rigging needed no urging to leap for the lifeboat. One of them fell on top of one of his rescuers and then slipped into the boiling sea, but he was almost immediately hauled to safety again. Then the lifeboat set about the dangerous task of reaching the men trapped on the wheelhouse of the sloop, and once again, after many attempts, their efforts met with success. The only other crew members of the *Pomona* were three men who had earlier been washed over the side. Two of them somehow managed to scramble ashore. The third, the *Pomona's* captain, was lost.

Heavy seas swept the *Kentwell* lifeboat throughout the rescue and the boat took a fearful pounding in the shallow, broken water. The crew told on their return of three great smashing waves in particular. In the trough of one of these the *Kentwell* actually struck the bottom.

The heroism displayed by the Lowestoft life-boatmen in carrying out the *Pomona* rescue received little publicity at the time, but official recognition followed. The Royal National Life-boat Institution awarded Coxswain Swan a bar to the silver medal he already held. A bronze medal went to the second coxswain, George Ayers, and each man in the crew received a certificate in recognition of his part in the rescue.

Another outstanding rescue in which Coxswain Swan played a major role came in October, 1922, when the North Sea would have claimed more lives but for the incredible bravery and seamanship of the local lifeboatmen. The 2300-ton steamer *Hopelyn* fell victim to the treacherous sandbanks off the East Anglian coast in a north-easterly gale after the vessel's steering gear had failed. Two anchors were not enough to stop the vessel being driven before the wind and at 9.30 p.m. on the evening of Thursday, October 19th, the *Hopelyn* ran hard aground on the North Scroby Sands.

Heavy seas combined with an ebbing tide to break the back of the stranded steamer and the 24 members of the crew soon found themselves in a position of the gravest peril. A radio call for help from the *Hopelyn* was followed by a final message that the ship was beginning to break up. Immediately after this signal the wireless mast was carried away and tumultuous seas began smashing completely over the vessel. The crew attempted to seek refuge in the saloon under the bridge, but then made for the tiny Marconi room, only some 12ft. square but situated in the highest part of the ship.

The first attempt at rescue was mounted by the *Kentwell* lifeboat, then based at Gorleston, which was taken out of harbour by the tug *George Jewson* after news that the Caister life-boat was unable to launch. Darkness and the raging seas frustrated any attempt by the lifeboatmen, under Coxswain William Fleming, to get alongside the wreck that night. And when morning came only the amidships section of the *Hopelyn* was still showing above water, and there was no sign of life on board.

After standing by for a further two hours the lifeboat moved away with the attendant tug and returned to Gorleston. The trapped men on board the *Hopelyn* saw the *Kentwell* leave, but at that time were unable to do anything to attract attention. An hour after the *Kentwell* berthed, however, there was a report from Caister that a flag had been seen on board the wreck, and Coxswain Fleming at once called his crew together to put out for Scroby once more. Yet again the weather and the hazardous position of the wreck frustrated a rescue bid by the Gorleston men but while they continued attempts to get alongside the *Hopelyn* orders were going out on shore for the launch of the Lowestoft motor lifeboat *Agnes Cross*.

Coxswain Swan was at the helm as the lifeboat ploughed into heavy seas for Gorleston to take on board the District Inspector, Mr. Carver. Then course was set for Scroby Sands. The *Agnes Cross* approached the wreck just as the Gorleston boat was pulling away, and Coxswain Fleming made a daring leap across to the Lowestoft lifeboat to put his view that he thought it impossible to carry out the rescue on the falling tide.

Coxswain Swan agreed with his colleague, and later recorded in his log: "As our boat draws several inches more than the *Kent-well* I did not think much of our chances that night, especially as he said the side plates of the wrecked vessel were sticking out. We could see no sign of life and it would have been unsafe to go too near for fear of having our air tanks burst".

Both the Gorleston and Lowestoft lifeboats, therefore, turned again for the shore, while on board the crippled *Hopelyn* the crew settled themselves as best they could for another night of terror.

The life-boatmen, meanwhile, had not the slightest intention of giving up, and plans were put in hand for the *Agnes Cross* to be used in conjunction with the Gorleston No. 2 lifeboat in yet a further desperate attempt to reach the wreck.

In the early hours of Saturday morning the weather worsened still further, and it was finally decided that the Lowestoft boat should set out alone at 4.30 a.m. Five members of the Lowestoft crew all skippers of fishing vessels had to return to their home port overnight. Seven Gorleston men, including Coxswain Fleming, joined the ten regular Lowestoft crew members for the rescue bid.

On this occasion as the wreck was approached the life-boatmen saw that though the *Hopelyn's* bow and stern were under water a white flag was being waved from the bridge as an indication that men were still alive on board. Coxswain Swan immediately reached a decision as to what had to be done. He steered in to the *Hopelyn* from the lee side, and then ordered an anchor to be put out before going astern towards the ripped and jagged side of the steamer.

The men on the *Hopelyn* were quick to seize their brief chance as the lifeboat nestled momentarily against the steamer in the only clear space left. Ropes were hastily thrown down from the bridge, and the 24 survivors scrambled down into the lifeboat. As the *Agnes Cross* sheered away from the wreck it was swept by a gigantic sea, but somehow everybody on board managed to retain their hold. The lifeboat's powerful 60 h.p. engine never faltered as it was tested to the limit in forcing the *Agnes Cross* clear. Danger was not quite over for the life-boatmen and the survivors, however. The anchor cable paid out from the *Agnes Cross* fouled the wreck, and the rope had to be cut before the lifeboat could get completely clear and make triumphantly for Yarmouth.

It was an outstanding rescue, and those who had remained safe on shore while it was carried out were quick to show their appreciation of the valiant efforts of the life-boatmen. As the *Agnes Cross* moved up river crowds cheered from the shore and from the many berthed fishing vessels. And as the survivors thankfully clambered ashore at Hall Quay they turned and gave three hearty cheers for their rescuers. Coxswains Swan and Fleming were each awarded the O.B.E. and the gold medal of the Royal National Life-boat Institution for their part in the rescue. And medals and certificates went also to the other men who had crewed the two lifeboats.

In both the *Pomona* and *Hopelyn* rescues the sole adversary for the local men was the unyielding North Sea itself. But in times of war there have been other adversaries, equally unyielding, and Lowestoft fishermen have always acquitted themselves bravely whenever danger has threatened.

One such man who will always have an honoured place in the history of his native town was Skipper Tom Crisp, whose bravery in action against a German submarine won him the posthumous award of the Victoria Cross. Skipper Crisp was in command of *H.M.A.S. (His Majesty's Auxiliary Smack) Nelson* when the action which was to cost him his life began about noon on August 15, 1917.

Working with the *Nelson* was another smack, the *Ethel and Willie* and the two were about 40 miles off Lowestoft when a submarine surfaced away to the north west. "Clear for action, submarine", ordered Skipper Crisp. And he had just given the command when a shot fell about a hundred yards away on the port bow. The *Nelson's* trawling gear was let go at once and the vessel's 13-pounder gun was ready to fire in a matter of seconds. The other smack was only armed with a 3-pound gun and the submarine concentrated its attack on the *Nelson* with deadly effect.

The fourth shot fired by the Germans sent a shell through the *Nelson's* port bow just below the water line. The seventh shell struck Skipper Crisp himself, passed through his side, through the deck and out through the side of the ship.

The skipper's 18-year-old son, Tom, who was the *Nelson's* mate, at once took charge of the tiller and the firing continued, though it was apparent that the *Nelson* was sinking and could not stay afloat much longer. One member of the eight-man crew, the gun layer, went to the skipper to see if he could render first-aid, but it was obvious that he was mortally wounded. And it was at this time that Skipper Crisp's indomitable courage came to the fore. 'It's all right boy, do your best", he said and, to his son, "Send a message off". This was the message, sent off from the smack by carrier pigeon: *"Nelson* being attacked by submarine. Skipper killed. Send assistance at once".

All this time the smack was settling lower in the water, and when only five rounds of ammunition were left young Tom Crisp went to his father and heard him say: "Abandon ship, throw the books overboard". Skipper Crisp was asked if he should be lifted into the boat, but his answer was, "Tom, I'm done. Throw me overboard". But he was in too bad a condition to be moved, and was left there on the deck while his crew took to the small boat. About a quarter of an hour later the *Nelson* went down by the head.

Young Tom took charge of the boat and, while the submarine turned its fire on the other smack, they were able to slip away from the scene. All night and the following day the survivors kept going, and after another night Tom managed to secure the boat to a buoy. And there they stayed until they were sighted and picked up by *H.M.S. Driad.*

Skipper Crisp was one of only two fishermen to be awarded the Victoria Cross during the first World War. His son Tom was awarded the D.S.M. and so achieved a remarkable distinction in that there is no other instance of a son being highly decorated at the same time and in the same circumstances as his father.

When the official announcement was made of the awards the "Lowestoft Journal" recorded that there was "not a finer or more splendidly tragic story in the annals of our sea fighting" than that of the smack *Nelson.*

Nothing, the paper said, could ever break the spirit of the local fishermen. And what finer epitaph than that could there be for the whole of that sturdy breed of men who are always ready to answer the call of duty and to face any danger? The Roaring Boys have never sought honours and awards for what they have done but each and every one deserves recognition for the bravery and skill which is their birthright.

END OF AN ERA

The year 1961 saw the end of an era at Lowestoft the end of the age of steam in the history of the fishing fleet. Earlier that year *Prime* went to the breaker's yard, Sir Lancelot, the fishery protection vessel, was replaced by *Clione,* leaving Lizzie West as the sole remaining steam vessel at the port. It was announced that she had been sold, It was 64 years before that the first steam-powered fishing vessel was built at Lowestoft. and the coming of steam brought the port to a peak of prosperity'. Though steam came earlier to the Northern port, Lowestoft can claim the first efficient steam drifter. She was the *Consolation,* a wooden vessel built for Catchpole's by Chambers & Colby in 1897. She soon proved her worth, catching in her first season twice the average number of herring as the rest of the fleet.

She was followed two years later by *Test* and *Adventure,* built by Sam Richards. The boat owners who had regarded steam- with some suspicion, were convinced. By 1903 there were 100 steamers working out of the port and five years later the figure had soared to 226.

It was the drifters which led the change-over to steam, and by 1918 not one sailing drifter was left. The trawlers were slower to adopt steam and the last of the sailing smacks did not disappear until the second world war. By that time oil power was beginning to sound the death knell of steam.

The year 1931 was a landmark in the age of steam and Lowestoft. In that year the Merbreeze, a 93 ft. drifter/trawler, was completed probably the last coal-burner built for the port.

She is still fishing out of Lowestoft. but like so many of the later steamers she has been converted to diesel power.

The past 60 years have seen the passing of sail and of steam .in Lowestoft. Today the diesel reigns supreme. What will be the next revolution -- atomic power?

LOWESTOFT JOURNAL NOTES

SNODS

Following my note on the "girls" engaged in the kippering, I was taken to task by a King's Lynn reader, who writes: about the correct name for the finger-rags worn by the girls; 'It is only 50 years since I first went to work in Yarmouth so I wouldn't know what went on before that but I have never seen *a* Scots 'girl' with rubbers on, on a Sunday. For evenings and the Sabbath they mostly wore made-to- measure boots and for work not rubbers but Baltic boots with pegged soles. Their finger rags were not snods' but 'gutty cogs.' I stand to be corrected but I have verified these facts with my wife, who incidentally is, or was a Shetland fishergirl who has worked in Lerwick. Lowestoft and Yarmouth, has kippered in Edinburgh and worked with white fish in Aberdeen"

My correspondent may well be right with regard to the footwear that was worn by the girls, but I still maintain that the correct name for their finger rags is "snods." "Gutty cogs" I have always understood to be the small wooden receptacles that were used for the entrails of the herring during gutting. When there were still gutting yards the west side of the river at Yarmouth I have a hazy recollection of seeing them in use there.

Returning to footwear for a moment, a curer to whom I spoke on the herring market told me that he could remember the girls wearing rubber boots, these, of course, would be very dangerous on the slippery working surfaces there was no compensation for accidents years ago but the girls dealt with this by having leather soles fitted as soon as they bought the boots.

This season has been a poor one for the herring curers, and for many of those who hope to gain at least a reasonable return from the East Anglian voyage. During the past week it has been a dispiriting experience to walk through the Fish Market at Lowestoft. The drifters that have brought in herring have returned to sea very quickly, and most afternoons in the last few days there has not been *a* single drifter tied up.

A good November fishing is needed to change the picture.

(From the Lowestoft Journal of Saturday, November 1ˢᵗ 1958)

LOWESTOFT

Talk to practically any local older fishermen about their years at sea and they will tell you how they started as smack cooks at the tender age of 11 or 12 , earning a few shillings a week. It did them no harm, they will tell you, and many of them certainly did well in later life, rising to become skippers and even boat-owners in their own right.

One wonders how contented the crew were to have their meals prepared by an 11-year-old youngster with no more knowledge of cooking than could be imparted by a few hasty lessons from mother.

One old fisherman told me that his first efforts as a cook were not appreciated by the crew. He had made stew and dumplings and the crew had grumbled a bit about the curious colour of the dumplings and the saltiness of the gravy. It was not until all the stew was finished that the truth came out he had used water from the harbour for all his cooking!

"When they found out they put me in the harbour." he recalled. "I nearly went home that day, but I stayed on and it wasn't long before I got out of the galley and on to the deck."

It was not a very auspicious start to a fishing career, but it certainly, did him no harm he went on to become one of the Port's leading skippers.

But of course, once a youngster had mastered the art of cooking fish and making tea, he was well away. They were the staple diet of the fishermen In those days and still are to a great extent today. I believe- trawler tea is a beverage all on its own. bearing little resemblance to the stuff one sips elegantly out of a china cup at home. The test of a good brew of trawler tea is does it leave a good thick brown stain round the inside of the mug?

With a pint or two of this and plenty of fish they seem ready for anything which brings me back to the old argument how many herring can a fisherman eat at one sitting?' I am told that a "comfortable" number is a dozen. but that is by no means the limit I wonder if there is a champion herring or fish eater of the Lowestoft fleet?

TEA

Writing about tea, and touching on the strong trawler brews, gained me an invitation to a cup from the most unusual pot I have ever seen and, incidentally, to hear the story of a coincidence.

The teapot belongs to a friend of mine who bought it a few days ago after seeing it in the window of a "junk" shop in Ipswich. It is the "Patent Syp Teapot" made by the famous Wedgwood firm for an exhibition some 50 years ago.

The peculiarity of it is that it incorporates a special straining device which certainly gave my friend and family a leafless cup of tea

To begin with, the pot can be stood in two positions upright in the normal position, or on its back. Running across the inside of the pot is a perforated shelf- With the pot standing on its back, the tea is put on the shelf and the boiling water added. After a proper time for infusion, the pot is turned right way up, leaving the tea leaves on the shelf

HOW'S THAT

Only a few of these teapots were made by Wedgewood's for this special exhibition at the beginning of the century, and my friend, who takes something of an interest in china. saw one for the first time at the home of a neighbour a few weeks ago

" I was intrigued by it." he told me. "never having seen, or even heard of. anything like it before. Two days later I happened to be in Ipswich and passing the time waiting for a bookshop to open I looked in the window of a 'junk' shop and there was its sister-pot. How's that for a coincidence? "

He promptly bought the pot for 7s. 6d and counts it as one of his lucky finds. It would be interesting to know whether there are any more of these patent teapots in existence.

WILL YOU SEE THE MAYFLY ON JUNE 24th?

I much enjoyed Graham Payne's story of his encounter with a phantom coach on the old Latymere Dam bridge. It happened one dark night in 1942 when Graham - sixteen at the time - was cycling home to Kessingland after visiting his girlfriend in Benacre. "It was about midnight as I rode down the hill on the Benacre side of the dam" he recalled. "I first saw what I thought was a car coming towards me, but when I got nearer I saw it was an old-fashioned horse-drawn coach, but when I reached the bridge there was nothing there at all! As I rode across the bridge I felt as though I had passed through an ice-cold patch. I was scared to death and rode home like a bat from hell."

Midnight on a winter's night seems to be a favourite time for such apparitions to make their appearance.

Kessingland's 'Grey Lady of Wash Lane' used, it is said, to turn up at about that time, but she has not been seen for many years!

But there are quite a number of summer ghosts in the area, notably that of the wherry, Mayfly, which is supposed to appear on Oulton Broad every year on June 24th. The visitation is quite a spectacular one - a full-sized wherry under full sail which appears promptly at 12.30am and spends half an hour sailing round the Broad. It all began in 1851, so it is claimed, when a Bank in Beccles, needing to shift £400,000 in cash to Yarmouth, chartered the Mayfly, under her skipper 'Blood Stephenson' to make the delivery. He was a notorious character and, as if the money was not enough temptation, the Bank also sent the daughter of one of the Directors, Millicent Dormay, on the trip! It all proved too much for 'Blood', who took the wherry out onto the North Sea. Millicent repulsed his advances and cabin boy Bert Entwhistle sprang to her defence. The struggle ended with both 'Blood' and Millicent lying dead on deck. Bert made his getaway in a small boat and he thought his ordeal was over when he spotted a sail. When the vessel got nearer he recognised her as the Mayfly, gleaming with a horrible phosphorescence - already a hell ship destined to sail the seven seas for ever. It must have lost track of the seven seas because it eventually turned up on Oulton Broad with 'Blood' cursing his fate and Millicent screaming for help. So the legend of the phantom wherry was born and was taken so seriously that in the 1930s no fewer than four learned societies kept vigil on the Broad. But the Mayfly failed to appear, nor has it been seen since.

Another summer ghost is supposed to appear at Burgh St. Peter's Church every May 2nd. It is the story of a man who sold his soul to the devil and then failed to keep his part of the bargain. Adam Morland was a man who longed for riches and when a benevolent old man offered him a fortune in return for his soul, he eagerly accepted. Adam Morland died before the devil could claim his part of the bargain, but it is said that on the anniversary of his demise a skeleton waits outside the church - hoping to collect his soul for the devil. This collector of souls has not been seen for a great many years, but it might be worth a visit to St. Peter's one May 2nd., just in case! So long as one does not meet a benevolent old gentleman and accept his offer of instant wealth!

FIRE

Down the centuries the most feared hazard in cities, towns and villages across the country was that of fire. With little in the way of fire-fighting equipment, little could be done to stem the flames. As a last resort, buildings which had not yet been engulfed, were torn down to create fire breaks, but this rarely proved effective.

In March 1644, Lowestoft suffered 'the greatest calamity that has ever afflicted it.'"a most violent fire which burned down so many houses as could not be rebuilt for above £10,000" according to the historians. Some 15 years later, Southwold was devastated by so disastrous a fire that within four short hours Town Hall, Market Place, Prison, shops, warehouses and 238 dwelling houses were utterly consumed, to the ruin of more than 300 families, the total loss being estimated at over £40,000.

It was not until late in the last century that fire-fighting equipment became more general. It was a devastating fire on Lowestoft's South Pier, in 1874, in which the Reading Room was totally destroyed, that prompted the town to invest in one of the new powerful steam pumps to supply its hoses. It proved even more powerful than had been anticipated! Crowds turned out to watch a demonstration of it in action. The show took place on the Royal Plain. After a timid start, with the pump on low power, the Firemen gained confidence and called for full power. With it going full steam the firemen discovered that they could not hold the writhing hoses and the crowd became soaked. At this the Mayor, in full robes and regalia, stepped forward calling on the firemen to switch off. Unfortunately by this time, the firemen had lost control and the Mayor was hit full on by one of the jets and was sent bowling along the gutter. Soaking wet, he was persuaded to go into the Royal Hotel for a change of clothing and a tot or two to warm him up. With the Mayor safely out of the way, the firemen embarked on yet another demonstration of their new toy. They would, they said, send a jet of water clean over the Hotel. They nearly made it, but not quite. The jet just failed to make it over the roof and instead, smashed a number of the windows, including that of the bedroom where the Mayor had taken shelter. When his dripping and irate figure appeared at the broken window, the firemen decided to call it a day, put out the boiler fire and discreetly went home! It was, declared the townspeople, the best entertainment they had ever seen!

The new steam pump certainly made an impact on fires after this, but there were still devastating blazes. In 1903 Swannells Maltings were burned out in a fire which raged for 24 hours and in the following year the Oil Mills in Commercial Road were gutted.

The Great Southwold Fire of 1659 destroyed much of the centre of the town, but it was a catastrophe which eventually lead to the creation of the town's most attractive features, its charming and popular greens

BENACRE DISASTER

Over the years I have been in the habit of jotting down in my diary the dates of newsworthy events in Kessingland and the neighbouring towns and villages. Some of them have been dramatic, but none more so than the fires which destroyed two stately homes in the area.

It was on February 20 1926 that the Lowestoft Journal - under the headline "The Benacre Disaster" - reported the huge fire which destroyed Benacre Hall and most of its contents.

"There will be very general sympathy with Sir Thomas and Lady Gooch in the loss by fire of their ancestral home and most of its contents" commented the Journal.

"Many thousands of people have been given infinite pleasure when Sir Thomas unreservedly threw open his grounds for annual flower shows, sports and other events" the Journal went on, "The fine mansion with its priceless oil paintings of bygone members of the family was always a great attraction. Now it is only a smoke-blackened shell with the beautiful stone colonnaded porch and frieze, surmounted by the Gooch crest and motto, standing as a remnant of its former glory.

"Local residents worked frantically to salvage portraits, furniture and silver plate, but such was the blaze that they were only partially successful".

The Hall was later rebuilt.

This was not the first stately home in the area to go up in flames. Henham Hall, seat of the Earls of Stradbroke was totally destroyed along with its contents in 1773. It was at 4.00am that the fire was discovered and it very quickly became a raging inferno. Before nightfall the mansion, built in the reign of Elizabeth I, had been reduced to a smouldering ruin.

The blame for the devastation was laid at the door of the Earl's butler!

It was alleged that "While robbing the cellar during his master's absence his candle set fire to sawdust in one of the wine bins." The butler, it was said, later fled to Devonshire, assumed a new name and was never heard of again!

Twenty years later a new hall was built and it remained the home of the Stradbroke family until the middle of this century when Lord Stradbroke decided that it was far too large for modern use - and, in any case, it had been built in the Victorian style which was not to his taste. The Hall was offered for sale, the hope being that it might be bought for a school or some other institution. There were no takers, so it was decided to sell the Hall, and its contents, lock, stock and barrel, a condition being that whoever bought the Hall should demolish it within a year.

The stage was set for what must rank as "The Sale of the Century".

Bidders flocked from all parts of the country. No fewer than six contractors bid against each other for the fabric of the mansion which, it was estimated, contained 100 000 feet of timber, 35 tons of leadwork and a million red and white bricks. It was finally knocked down for £3 10s.

Priceless antiques were, by present day prices, going for a song. The State Four-Poster bed in which King George V slept when a guest at the Hall, attracted a great deal of interest.

"Its domed head was carved and gilded and was surrounded by cherubs" said a description. "The foot was carved and supported by three-quarter length female figures and the bed had rich brocade trimmings"

Despite the wide interest, it sold for a mere £14!

Among the other lots, a mahogany long case clock for £15, a Sutherland table for £11 and 17 old leather fire buckets for £16. There was more spirited bidding for the garden ornaments and wrought iron gates which fetched around £70 a pair.

A suite of mahogany doors from the staterooms and principal bedrooms - described as "The gems of the House" was bought for £1,000 by the London Mercer's Company and were used in the rebuilding of their Hall which was destroyed in the Blitz.

The Butchers' Company, who's Hall had been another victim of the bombing, went home with a period chimney piece in white marble for a mere £80.

A cantilever stone staircase went for £31, and the Ballroom floor, oak inlaid and complete with its sprung floor sold for £30.

Truly "The Sale of the Century".

MURDER OF THE VILLAGE CONSTABLE

The office of Parish Constable is one of our most ancient institutions, dating back to the 12th. century. Down the ages he has been responsible for maintaining law and order. And not only that, for this unpaid officer appointed by the Parish Vestry meeting, was originally saddled with a long and bewildering list of duties. In addition to the provision of Watch and Ward, he also had to keep the village stocks and cage in good repair; inspect alehouses; maintain the parish armour and arms; submit lists of parishioners who failed to attend church; and finally, and not least, to care for the parish bull and to ensure it was available when required!

It was not a popular job and most nominees contrived to avoid the office either by paying someone to take their place, or by the production of what was known as a 'Tyburn Ticket'. This certificate, granted to anyone who successfully prosecuted a felon, gave immunity to being selected for a public office. It was transferable to any other person. Consequently, it was very saleable, fetching up to £30.

Although the village constable was often incompetent and feeble, the old system staggered along until the late 18th. century when, with the growing industrial revolution, there were many outbreaks of riots against rising food prices and the new turnpike roads. They graphically demonstrated the absence of any effective means of keeping order.

London saw the introduction of the Bow Street Runners and in 1829 Sir Robert Peel organised the Metropolitan Police. Its success led to similar Forces being established in many parts of the country. The East Suffolk Police Force was formed in 1840, adopting the uniform of the Met - a beaverskin top hat, blue swallow-tailed coat with white duck trousers for summer and blue in winter, boots, truncheon, rattle and lantern.

The top hat was a tall, stout affair with a leather top and braced inside with cane and wire supports. This was not only to protect the wearer from blows to the head, but the hat could also be used as a stepping stone in scaling a high wall or fence.

Sounds a good idea, but it also produces a curious predicament. How did the constable get back over the wall to retrieve his helmet?

The top hat also proved somewhat cumbersome and was likely to fall off during a chase or struggle. It was quickly replaced by a shorter model and was eventually changed to the traditional helmet which was based on that of the Prussian Army.

The violence of the towns quickly spread to the countryside and in July 1844 the East Suffolk Constabulary saw the first murder of one of its officers - Kessingland's village bobby James McFadden. He had surprised three men who were breaking into a barn at Gisleham. They were well known to him - William Howell, aged 28: his brother Walter, 21: and Israel Shipley, 38. McFadden immediately confronted the three men and, although threatened with a gun by William Howell, went forward to arrest them. As he did so Howell fired, seriously injuring him in the thigh. Despite his injury, McFadden staggered to his feet and again tried to arrest the men. William Howell and Shipley then knocked him to the ground where they kicked him savagely before the trio made their getaway. McFadden managed to crawl to a nearby farmhouse and raise the alarm, but a little later he died at his home in Kessingland.

In the hue and cry that followed, the Chief Constable asked the Home Secretary to sanction the issue of firearms to all his constables. This was refused, but authority was given for them to carry cutlasses at night, but only if two Justices of the Peace were satisfied that they were required 'for their personal protection in the performance of their duties'.

Luckily, the three men were tracked down and arrested without further resistance. They were tried at Ipswich Assizes. William Howell, who had fired the fatal shot, was sentenced to death. So were the other two men, but their sentences were commuted to transportation for life to the penal settlement on Norfolk Island off the Australian coast.

There was no reprieve for William Howell. He was hanged outside Ipswich Gaol. A huge crowd gathered for his public execution and heard him go to his death still protesting his innocence.

As for the other two, they had been sent to a living hell of starvation and brutality. Few survived. A Marine, John Easty, who served on Norfolk Island recorded in his diary the horror of the place: "A pore mersable (miserable) place and all manners of cruelties and oppression used by the Governor flogging and beating people to Death that it is better for the pore unhappy Creatures to be hanged almost than come under the command of such Tyrants".

This, then, was where those two Kessingland men ended up. No more is known of their fate. Perhaps they came to regret the 'mercy' which had been shown them and that they had not joined William Howell on the scaffold.

SWAN SONG OF THE ROYAL BIRD

The announcement some years ago by a West Country hotel that roast swan was to appear regularly on its menu aroused a certain amount of interest - but also a good deal of indignation among people who obviously did not regard the swan as an edible dish.

Swans are such ornamental birds that they have almost ceased to be regarded as a source of food, but for hundreds of years roast swan was looked upon as a great delicacy.

Henry VIII was so fond of the dish that he decreed that all swans on the Thames were the property of the Crown. He made a couple of exceptions, granting two City of London Companies - the Dyers and Weavers - the right to take swans to be served at their annual banquets.

The Great Hospital in Norwich was also permitted to take swans from the River Bure. The sale of these swans enabled the Hospital to continue its charitable work and to finance its Almshouses.

It was from the Great Hospital that the Wherry Hotel at Oulton Broad obtained a swan when, in 1862, a group of musicians who met regularly at the Wherry decided that they would like to try roast swan at their annual supper. The innovation proved so popular that it became an annual event, known for some obscure reason, as 'The Tradesmen's Dinner'.

Along with the swan came the cooking instructions:

"Take three rounds of beef, beat fine in a mortar

Put into the swan, that is when you've caught her."

The recipe also included peppers, mace, nutmeg, Port wine and hot red currant jelly. There was a warning that enjoyment of the dish depended much on culinary skill and that "The untrained palate often prefers more common Birds"!

This annual supper continued without a break till 1914 when it was ended by the outbreak of war. It was revived with great success in 1929 and it seemed that it would once again be an annual event at the Wherry. It was, indeed held the following year and there was a good turnout, but then it was allowed to lapse. Because, perhaps, public taste was changing, it was never held again. As far as the Wherry was concerned, this was, one might say, its "Swan Song".

In the meantime the Great Hospital continued to send out its boatmen on the annual swan-upping to mark the beaks of the cygnets with the distinguishing marks of the various owners. A proportion of the birds were taken back to be fattened for the Christmas trade in a specially built pool known as the Swan Pit. The second World War, rationing and a shortage of grain put an end to a tradition which had continued since the 14th. century. The swans had been in demand all over the country during the run-up to Christmas - and some went even further afield. The Duke of Norfolk used to send them to the Pope in Rome.

This Christmas, I imagine, few roast swans will grace the festive board, preference being given to "more common birds".

Owners of swans on the Broads had their own marks to identify their particular birds. This was the mark of William Holmes in 1882.

A KESSINGLAND CHRISTMAS CRACKER

There is a miscellany of customs and beliefs at this festive season of the year. Some go back centuries. Others, like the sending of Christmas Cards, are of comparatively modern origin. It is estimated that this year well over 1000 million cards will be sent out in this country alone, bringing joy not only to the recipients, but to the Post Office, the printers and to the many charities which benefit from the sale of their own special cards.

This avalanche of cards owes its origins to the laziness of one man, Sir Henry Cole, founder of the Victoria and Albert Museum. It had been his habit to write Christmas letters to his friends, but in the run-up to Christmas 1843 he did not feel up to this annual chore. So he asked an artist friend, J C Horsley, to design a greetings card. One thousand of the cards were printed

and sent to friends of the two men. It was some twenty years, however, before the idea caught on commercially, but by 1870 six firms were printing and selling cards. The adoption of the idea by the Royal Family quickly added to the cards' popularity.

The enormous growth in the card industry is usually credited to that first Christmas Card, but oddly enough commercially printed Valentine Cards were on sale long before Sir Henry had his bright idea.

The boom in Valentine Cards had been boosted by the introduction of the Penny Post. So large were deliveries of these cards that one magazine commented: "The weary Postman sinks beneath a load of embarrassment not his own!"

Not all these early Valentines, however, expressed compliments or vows of undying love. There were the notorious 'Venomous Valentines' which were sent by spiteful people to spinsters and old maids pointing out their defects and failings!

Christmas Cards however, kept to the theme of 'Goodwill to all' and by the turn of the century the familiar scenes of stage coaches with loads of merrymakers, robins, holly, blazing log fires and Christmas Puddings had been established as the favourite themes.

Times have changed but the robin has maintained his place as one of the most popular - and rightly so. Legend has it that the robin gained his crimson breast when trying to draw a thorn from the Crown of Thorns. A drop of our Lord's blood fell on him, staining his breast feathers for ever.

Mistletoe, too, has long had a place on our cards and in the home, though, because of its pagan origins, many churches will not tolerate it amongst the Christmas greenery. An exception is York Minster where, by ancient tradition, a sprig is placed on the High Altar.

So mistletoe is largely confined to the domestic scene, but those who kiss under the mistletoe should remember that there are certain rules to be obeyed - one kiss for each berry. When all the berries have gone, the kissing has to stop. There seems, however, to be no prohibition on the introduction of a new bunch!

Midnight Mass has, in recent years, become more and more popular in an increasing number of parishes, though the walk home in the dark is not welcomed by those with a nervous disposition.

They can take comfort from the assurance that evil spirits are rendered harmless during this holy time. Christmas is a time not only of special services, good cheer and presents, but also of good luck. There is an old saying that to eat 12 mince pies between Christmas and Twelfth Night ensures 12 happy months during the coming year. They should, however, have been baked by different cooks, hence the old custom of friends and neighbours exchanging their home-baked mince pies. Lucky, too, the housewife who bakes a loaf on Christmas Day. It will not only prevent the home being struck by lightning, but will also clear the place of rats and mice!

I must say that I take this with a pinch of salt, as I do the old belief that a child born on Christmas Day will be immune to death by hanging!

This was the card which started it all in 1843 - over 150 years ago - when Sir Henry Cole was too lazy to write his usual Christmas letters to his many friends

The price of Christmas Cards seems to have risen annually over the past 150 years, but way back in 1914 you could have bought this local effort featuring Lowestoft Esplanade for just one penny. A dealer sold it to me for £2.50! Ironically it first appeared in the year which saw the outbreak of the First World War - it was printed in Saxony, then a small kingdom of Germany!

We leave Kessingland enjoying the first Christmas Cards and basking in the heyday of the fishing bonanza, but change was to come, when the slow decline of the industry forced the village to adapt to an ever-changing situation, with the tourist industry bringing the employment to both men and women whose forefathers had gained a living from the harvest of the land or the sea. We continue the story in Part Three of the Village History, to be entitled: *The Most Easterly Village in England, Where the Sun Shines First.*